How to be a black-belt manager

How to be a black-belt manager

Martial arts and the art of managing people

Robert Pater

THORSONS PUBLISHING GROUP

First published in US by Destiny Books 1988.
This edition published 1989.

British Library Cataloguing in Publication Data

ISBN 0-7225-1625-8

Published by Thorsons Publishers Limited, Wellingborough, Northamptonshire,
NN8 2RQ, England.

Printed and bound in Great Britain by Mackays of Chatham PLC, Kent

1 3 5 7 9 10 8 6 4 2

For Franz Pater
who taught me the power of gentleness

ACKNOWLEDGEMENTS

Thank you to the many who have helped this book come to be. To my colleague Robert Button for his creativity and support. He was instrumental in helping develop many of the concepts in this book. To those martial arts masters and management theorists who have blazed the paths. Special thanks to Mitsugi Saotome and mentor-friend Jack Gibb. To my primary martial arts instructors, John Clodig and Walter Muryasz, insightful and skilled men. To Don Fitch, who helped in the early stages. To Susan, for her love and continued support. To my daughter Kyra. To Carl and Lilian Greenberg for their faith and caring. To the clients and seminar participants who have successfully applied martial arts principles to their professional and personal lives. To Ehud Sperling and Leslie Colket, for their understanding during unusual circumstances, and Don Cioeta and Wendy Tilghman, who have been extremely helpful as editors. And to black-belt managers everywhere, dedicated to continually improving their professional skills and personal effectiveness, determined to become a positive force for organizational strength.

Contents

Introduction

Let me tell you a story about modern *karate*. It began in the following way. Gichin Funakoshi, as a small boy growing up in Okinawa, had the experience of watching his father being intimidated, bullied, and even beaten up. He loved his father, and was upset by his inability to intercede. He vowed to learn to protect himself from this kind of physical abuse and to pass on this skill to others.

He turned to the ancient martial art of *karate*, at that time a clandestine and inbred technique of warfare known as "the art of the open hand." It began as a traditional fighting form in which the hands and feet are used as weapons whereby unarmed men and women could combat armed horsemen. The flying kicks were designed to knock an attacker off a horse, and the punches to penetrate armour. (Weapons like *nunchaku* were originally a peasant tool for pounding rice.)

From traditional karate Funakoshi learned the arts of protection and defence, strategy on the battlefield, physical mastery, and self control. He also discovered that the martial arts are a means for transforming yourself, a technique for spiritual development also. They were about a way of living your life.

Funakoshi mastered the "art of the open hand." He taught it to others. But in Gichin Funakoshi's modern karate, it was no longer just the art of the few. He offered this effective teaching as a practical tool— for the many. He created a huge organization fuelled by loyal practitioners, which made a great impact on his own country and the world.

Funakoshi realized that at the heart of martial arts practice is the ability to deal with changing circumstances—to act and to react instantaneously, in the moment. He transformed karate into a system that would be useful in the modern world—to help people to be effective in daily life in all ways.

Making a practical application of the principles of the martial arts to one's way of life is part of its original spirit. And that is the point of my story. Emphasis on being practical and effective in action, focusing on your goals, and developing your full capabilities, mentally, physically, spiritually, and emotionally are at the heart of the martial arts.

I have found that these principles apply in business as well.

I began studying *jujitsu* and *aikido* in 1972. Since then, I have also practiced *tae kwon do, kenjutsu, tai chi,* and others. Once I got past the magical image of the martial artist as a superman, I was impressed by the beauty and efficiency of the disciplines: it makes more sense to direct overwhelming forces than to try to stop them. Control yourself and you can more readily influence situations, and so on. The martial arts became the basis of my own management style, and by 1976 I was incorporating their methods into my work as an organizational consultant.

The business world is one of swirling and continuous change, especially now. There is intense competition for resources; people are expected to do more with less. Mere survival is competitive, and to thrive is even more difficult. It depends on being able to anticipate and react to change, to assess conditions, to act decisively, and to be calm under pressure. In times of great change, the past is not duplicated by the future, so creative solutions and approaches are essential. To walk decisively through swirling change means the difference between survival and success.

It is crucial to be able to pool and synthesize human resources as well, and to work as part of a team instead of only individually. And it is essential to live a life that doesn't lose its meaning when you leave your job.

Self discipline, mastery of change, and working effectively with others are the principles behind this book. The martial arts techniques presented in the following chapters—many of which you are not likely to have seen elsewhere—are not merely esoteric or philosophical. They are simple and practical. They can help you cut through overwhelming problems at work, tap a reservoir of calmness during the trying times, and shatter obstacles to high performance.

You can apply these methods to develop your staff into stable, decisive, and innovative team players who can get the daily job done as well as focus on long-range opportunities.

These principles can help you develop your creativity, control, and effectiveness. They can help you enjoy your work more, and their benefits may also carry over into your personal life.

I have taught these techniques to thousands of people—from management trainees to upper-level executives—in a wide range of industries. Those who have used them report the same results: they work; conditions improve.

This is not a manual of Japanese management, nor is it a theoretical model. It is a step-by-step guidebook to transforming yourself into a manager with the skills and powers of an adept martial artist—self control, inner calmness under attack, and substained concentration on your goals.

It is also a guidebook to transforming your organization into a high-level, smoothly functioning organism—an organization harmoniously aligned and focused on reaching its most important goals and objectives.

THE STRATEGY

Martial arts practitioners learn in three stages.

First, students focus themselves. "The greatest warrior conquers himself first," contends an ancient martial arts maxim. You learn to control your own actions and reactions. You train to withstand pressure, not to freeze when you have to think fast and act strong.

In this initial stage of learning, the best students pay primary attention to themselves to accurately assess their own strengths and inefficiencies.

The second phase of development focuses on understanding others and the mechanisms that make them impressive allies, weak compatriots, or formidable enemies.

In the third stage, budding martial arts experts study the interaction between themselves and others. When I move so, how do you respond? And how can I counter your second attack? This stage is known as the field of change.

Black-belt managers develop in the same way as martial artists. Consequently, the book is organized according to the three stages of martial arts development. "You have to be disciplined with yourself before you can exercise good business discipline," according to Mario Bisio, a *karate* practitioner and owner of a clothing store chain. The self-mastery techniques in the first part of this book will help you increase your personal productivity, manage stress, and leverage a small amount of effort into large returns.

Success, wrote karate master Gichin Funakoshi, cannot be attained alone. Any person's time and power is limited. A wise manager enlists others in working toward organizational goals. The second section of this book highlights simple methods for harnessing rather than fighting people's natural reactions and emotions. You will learn techniques for developing a self-motivated staff, for being effective without wielding a big stick, for harnessing the power of dedication, and for using conflict for creativity.

Part III, Mastering Change, provides strategies for responding successfully to forces you cannot control, planning for organizational strength, and becoming an agent of productive change.

Each section includes experiences and observations of managers who have successfully applied martial arts principles in their organizations. Not all are martial arts practitioners, but they are all "black-belt managers." This doesn't mean they have mastered all the wisdom of management, but they have learned enough to begin applying the principles wisely.

New martial arts students are often surprised to see themselves training alongside advanced practitioners, all working on the same techniques. Why, they ask, are the brown and black belts still practising the same things? Real learning is not linear. Three people studying the same technique actually have different practices. The novice is working on basic footwork, the intermediate student on controlling balance, and the expert on subtleties of timing.

The same is true in developing management expertise. The methods in this book are as useful to the new supervisor as to the senior manager wishing to advance his or her skills.

Use this book wisely. If something doesn't make sense, throw it away, or put it aside for another time.

You may already have had many experiences of managing effectively. As you read, search not only for new techniques; look for explanations of what you already know. Look for the reasons behind your "lucky" accomplishments. You can also make quick improvements when you apply a skill to new areas. It is less a matter of knowing what to do than it is of remembering to do what you know.

Apply those techniques that make sense to you. Rereading other sections later on may provide further insights. You will see them with the eyes of a more advanced practitioner.

The ancient martial artists had a saying, "The best secrets keep themselves." There are no magical results without work. Inspiration, persistence, and patience open the door to powerful performance.

Through practice, martial artists actually reprogram their reflexes. While real life managerial expertise won't come from just reading a book, by applying these martial arts principles to your work, you can act and react with focus and control and foster a more dynamic and responsive organization. You can become a black belt in the art of managing.

Robert Pater
Portland, Oregon

PART I

MASTERING YOURSELF

The art of karate is a never ending quest for perfection . . . of developing the spirit and body to defeat your opponent . . . one's self.

Tak Kubota, *The Art of Karate*

Before the struggle, the victory is mine.

Mitsugi Saotome

CHAPTER ONE

How to Become a Black-Belt Manager

The true path of the Way applies at any time and in any situation.

Miyamoto Musashi, *A Book of Five Rings*

It didn't take me long to notice, first as a manager, and then as a consultant, how much energy was squandered in most organizations. I was disturbed to see how easily people became side-tracked by unimportant tasks and how shortsightedness endangered professional and organizational survival.

To my newly-minted supervisory mind, it didn't make any sense. Force was poorly applied, people appeared to operate with little control, and organizations were left, at best, wobbling toward their goals. This was not the way my organizational development studies said it should be, and certainly not in line with my desire for results.

Strategies that worked best on paper provided little solace. The strategies I trusted most were those of the martial arts (I was a student of two years at the time). They provided a source of principles and methods that were eminently effective in their own arena.

Sensing an important connection, I reflected on and read further about the martial arts view of the world, comparing it to the strategies of management experts who had proven results. I began using martial arts principles in my work wherever they seemed to fit, applying them during stressful times, in conflicts, and when I wanted to succeed in a particular area. Lo and behold—they worked.

Over the years, I injected these principles more frequently into my work with clients. With the martial arts as my inspiration, I developed physical metaphors for complex personal, interpersonal, and organizational events. I demonstrated these in seminars, and received strong positive responses. I was encouraged. My martial arts training was becoming a source for potent management strategies and methods.

At first some managers joked about it. Gradually, even traditional managers have come around, showing keen interest in what martial arts methods can do for them.

And the results can be most rewarding.

THE ART AND SCIENCE OF MANAGING AND MARTIAL ARTS

Like the martial arts, management is both science and art.

Early on, martial artists study how to execute a spinning kick without losing balance. Place the feet so, twist the upper body to gain momentum, and focus on a target point. That's the science.

Practise this form, the masters say, until you develop a feeling for the entire movement. Then you'll see where the technique really works and your timing will be truly effective. That's the art.

It's the same in managing. Good managers study the principles of management: worker motivation principles by Herzberg or Maslow; effective meeting dynamics; or such change management studies as how to reduce employee resistance to new systems. That's the science.

The best studies are done in a vacuum. They freeze the picture, and outside influences are stilled, not at all like the hectic, swirling patterns of most organizations.

Also, studies never predict what happens in individual circumstances.

And people are not predictable, or static. Have you ever thrashed out a problem and arrived at a meeting of minds with a colleague, only to find that early the next day, the rapport was no longer there? People do not pick up where they left off. Clearly, we behave in complex and changeable ways.

Unfortunately, "guaranteed" solutions rarely produce the expected results. Nothing works all the time in every circumstance. The art involves knowing which scientific principles are operating and how to apply them so you are not "going by the book." Real solutions must be artfully timed and adapted to different people and complex situations. Beginners study the science, but experts in both management and martial arts work more on the art.

Don't be lulled into unawareness or complacency. Things are never as smooth as they seem in a book or on the practice mat; situations never replicate themselves. The martial artist and the strong manager must always be ready to adapt.

Many people enthusiastically begin martial arts study and then just as quickly disappear. It may be that something else came up, but in many cases beginners are frustrated by an unrealistic quest for instant power. They seem to think they can go to a few classes and effortlessly become another Bruce Lee or Chuck Norris, or that just by copying the instructor, they will conquer fear and master grace.

It is not that easy. It takes years of dedicated practice. First you focus on understanding the science, then you get the feeling for the art. Ultimately, as Dan Inosanto wrote in *The Filipino Martial Arts*, "Knowledge comes from your instructors, wisdom comes from within."

Managers face the same temptation of looking to the outside for salvation. Many books, consultants, and seminars push the simple solutions, but business history is littered with the corpses of quick fixes.

Unfortunately, today's manager is still tempted. After spending much money and time on a quick fix, he usually finds that nothing has really changed, except that his confidence and credibility may have been compromised. Instead of seeking a magical, painless solution, black-belt managers, like martial artists, must study their science and develop their art. Some long-standing guidelines for developing mature martial artists is an excellent place to begin.

The Samurai Connection

Perhaps Miyamoto Musashi's guidelines for warriors can work for you as they have for business leaders throughout the world. In the late sixteenth century, Musashi wrote a book on swordsmanship. In the latter twentieth century, this slim treatise, *A Book Of Five Rings*, has become a business best seller, marketed as "the Japanese answer to the Harvard M.B.A."

As one story goes, an agent for a famous television talk programme tried to procure Musashi for a guest spot. The agent was nonplussed to discover that his coveted "hot celebrity" had been dead and buried for hundreds of years! Admittedly, Musashi was a great warrior, undefeated in all his fights, and this allowed him to live to a ripe age. Deemed a *kensei* ("sword saint") by his people, Musashi also transferred some of his battlefield insight to painting and other arts. His legacy was a legend and a book on martial strategy.

Why this much attention to Musashi now? It seems many managers recognize that martial strategy points toward winning business tactics. And in Japan, most business conglomerates are *samurai* (warrior class) families. Top managers practise martial arts and read Musashi for guidance in daily business affairs.

In *A Book Of Five Rings*, Musashi listed nine guidelines for developing warriors. These guidelines are also appropriate for developing black-belt managers.

1. Do not think dishonestly.
2. The Way is in the training.
3. Become acquainted with every art.
4. Know the ways of all professionals.
5. Distinguish between gain and loss in worldly matters.
6. Develop intuitive judgement and understanding for everything.
7. Perceive those things which cannot be seen.
8. Pay attention even to trifles.
9. Do nothing which is of no use.

When you understand them, these esoteric principles for the martial arts can readily promote black-belt managing.

1. DO NOT THINK DISHONESTLY

Walter Muryasz is a professional martial artist who specializes in training black belts in many systems. Muryasz has strong feelings about self-honesty. In *Precepts of the Martial Artist*, he writes, "The martial artist must always be on guard against self-delusion of any form. There is no room for it in the martial arts. Reality is the teacher and the test."

Miyamoto Musashi concurred; he described the Way of a warrior in *A Book of Five Rings* as "having no illusions in your heart, honing your wisdom and will power, sharpening your intuitive sense and your powers of observation day and night; when the clouds of illusion have cleared away, this is to be understood as the true path."

Martial arts instructor Robert Button believes illusions are created by fear of the unknown and by conditioning. Many people have lived with illusions so long that it is difficult for them to perceive what is real.

Black-belt managers are critically honest with themselves. They assess their strengths and limitations without excuse, and work to become *deeply* sure of themselves.

John Kerson was a senior manager at a wood products company. He had a booming career at one time. Hopping quickly through the ranks, from machine operator to supervisor, then from manager to plant manager, John made the leap into corporate headquarters.

He painfully discovered, however, that he was a fish out of water, and he couldn't do a good job in his present position. He didn't have a feeling for what he was doing, and his career was dying on the vine. He could probably continue—he knows how to cover himself well enough—but John is a black belt in the art of managing and being mediocre isn't good enough. So he is making his move. He gave himself six months to find a more suitable job, either internally (in a position where he can still be effective), or with another company. This is not an easy decision at all.

It's tempting to blame others and to try to escape personal responsibility. ("The job was a set-up from the beginning. Those other jokers fell down on the job. The market turned out to be too soft.") But you can't hide from yourself and still be effective. Somewhere, you know the truth, and ultimately, so will others.

In my experience, most people don't see themselves accurately. They exaggerate their strengths, and at the same time privately blow their weaknesses out of proportion. Too hard on themselves in one way, they're too soft in another. Both excesses are dangerous. To be effective, to continue to grow professionally, the manager has to know what he can really do.

Self-knowledge recognizes that every strength is a potential weakness and vice versa. A kick may be devastating if it lands, but it can also weaken balance. Managers with strong "people skills" can make disjointed staff jell into a smoothly working unit; but just as often, staff can become side-tracked in reverence for such a manager.

Knowing where you excel and where you founder is easier said than done. For the honest-thinking manager, it's essential to develop sources of external criticism that you can listen to without feeling threatened:

- Develop candour with colleagues and peers so that the norm is "To Tell It Like It Is." Get feedback from them on your strengths, weaknesses, and skill areas.

- Develop similar relationships with friends and family who can point out behaviour patterns that may also show up on the job. ("You never listen to me once you've made up your mind to do something.")

- Self-assessment tests may provide insight into your hidden strengths and weaknesses.

- Solicit feedback in the form of performance or quality indicators, attitude survey results, and others' responses to your actions.

- Watch how you receive feedback. Do you react defensively and seek to make excuses? These are danger signs. Can you absorb the feedback calmly—and consider how it can help you? Are you seeking approval or are you looking for ways to improve future performance?

- Maintain a *freshly informed* approach. Don't start from a conclusion. Remember you have limits. You don't have to know what to do in advance.

- Most important, listen to yourself. Watch inner voices that communicate mixed feelings.

Being honest with yourself means understanding that you have mixed feelings about everyone and everything. It's natural. Isn't the person you love most also someone you can't stand at times? And when you say you enjoy your job, the truth is that you may partly love it and partly dislike it. In most positions, there are tasks you look forward to and have-to-dos you wish you could avoid.

So it's natural to have mixed feelings about your job or about any specific action. In fact, it is dangerous to ignore them or rationalize them away. Know they are there, listen to them, and make them your allies. Mixed feelings help you in three ways:

- They help you reconsider before leaping into action. Sometimes actions appear totally favourable, especially when you want to be rescued from an uncomfortable situation. You may forget there is always a price to pay for precipitous action. If you are attuned to your doubting side, you may avoid leaping onto dangerous ground.

- They help you plan for contingencies. Seeing the possible down side will make your plans more realistic.

- They help you understand others who disagree with your position. When you understand dissenters, you'll have more influence with them.

Don't neglect to watch your interactions with others. In *The Tao of Jeet Kune Do*, Bruce Lee wrote, "To know oneself is to study oneself in action with another person." Others, especially difficult people, are your allies. There's nothing like a slow-tracking employee to upset an impatient manager. When you see yourself over-reacting, you can be thankful. Your weakness has been brought to the surface; you have an opportunity to work on becoming more patient, more disciplined—in short, a stronger manager.

Also develop a realistic view of your organization's strengths and limitations. It's great to be for the team, but not by blinding yourself to its weakness. If you can't see the weakness, you can't change it.

Finally, recognize that self-assessment is an ongoing activity. How many organizations have slipped from a position of strength because they rested on their laurels? Yearly self-assessments may provide historical perspective, but real strengthening comes from daily observation. Continue to monitor yourself and your organization honestly.

2. THE WAY IS IN THE TRAINING

The martial artist is dedicated to self-improvement through training. No one becomes a black belt without hours of weekly practice over several years. In his book *Karate-do: My Way of Life,* modern karate founder Gichin Funakoshi wrote, "Only through training will a person learn his own weaknesses . . . He who is aware of his weaknesses will remain master to himself in any situation."

The same is true for all black-belt managers I work with; efforts for self-improvement never end. The *Hagakure*, a respected martial arts source of unknown authorship, plainly states that once you begin to feel that you are a master, you are no longer making progress—self-development withers with self-satisfaction.

In training, you can't avoid correcting and doing the little things over and over again. "The martial artist is always training in one form or another," writes Walter Muryasz, the martial arts master. "In the beginning, the artist must practise form, *kata* (stylized combat against set invisible opponents), and movement. These cannot be rushed or neglected. They are the building blocks and cornerstones for efficiency later on in the art. It is the constant repetition of movements, form, and *kata* that will eventually effect a change in the artist's normal way of living. Years later, he will naturally move in a manner which makes his [martial] art a by-product of the way he moves. The art will not become a contrivance and he can then say, 'There is no difference between the way I lift my cup and the way I avoid a strike.' "

Training does not just take place in the *dojo* (training hall), which is a controlled and therefore artificial environment. Training is an ongoing process of attentively weaving the threads of book and classroom learning with real-life experience, adjusting when unsuccessful. In essence, training is a process of trial and self-correction. It's not mindless repetition, but the art and discipline of learning. This requires paying the utmost attention, as if your livelihood depended on it. Make a habit to practise applying to your work what you've read, seen, heard. Watch the results, then readjust accordingly.

This takes effort, even for an expert manager. Things rarely go as smoothly as described in a book, seminar, or anecdote about another company. And though it may be frustrating, this kind of on-the-job managerial training eventually creates natural, effective action.

A-dec's Phil Westover gives excellent seminars on effective use of training. He believes training is a waste of time *unless* there are realistic goals for the training. For example, it's not reasonable to expect a new student to fend off black belts after only one lesson. Nor will a two-week karate course remake someone's life.

Accurately distinguish between training's specific performance goals and the goals of the educational presentations (like Stress Control or Time Management) that are developmental in nature. The latter may raise morale and improve productivity in the long run, but rarely show immediate performance benefits.

Remember that for increased productivity, classroom training should be applied to the job, gradually and continuously. Many managers return from attending training seminars, ready to make work improvements, but are shot down by a change-resistant system. (Of course, a participant's unrealistic expectations of a quick change may be somewhat responsible for his plan's "bombing out.")

In the martial arts, it isn't true that "those who can, do; those who can't, teach." Teaching is an essential element of mastery. When you really understand, you can transmit the skill to others. In *Zen In The Art Of Archery*, Eugen Herrigel quotes an assistant *kyudo* (archery) instructor, "A great Master must also be a great teacher. With us the two things go hand in hand."

One of judo founder Professor Jigoro Kano's accomplishments was his development of a cadre of highly skilled students. This was also true for *aikido* Master Morehei Ueshiba, one of the greatest martial artists of the twentieth century.

Similarily, black-belt managers I have met relish training their staff, just as they continually advance their own skills and knowledge. When correctly applied, training is a powerful weapon for strengthening performance and raising the morale of those you work with.

3. BECOMING ACQUAINTED WITH EVERY ART

Every martial art system has its weaknesses and strengths. For example, in fighting, there are three "circles" of defence—the outside circle of the leg reach (kicking distance), the middle circle of the extended arm (punching distance), and the inner circle of the body (throwing, tripping distance). A predominantly kicking art like *tae kwon do* focuses on the outer circle; so students practise staying outside of their opponent's reach. The practitioners of this excellent Korean art are not as accustomed to a proficient grappling kind of attack. Judo artists, on the other hand, are more comfortable at moving in and going for the throw. But they are less practised in defending against a good kicking attack.

Not seeing your weaknesses can make you more vulnerable to attacks you haven't prepared for. What's the answer? Before you're in a tight situation, gain balance by exposing yourself to a complementary system. Then when you step on the battlefield, you can anticipate more realistically. You can best defend yourself against the long staff only after you have studied the weapon and its tactics. You no longer fight in a vacuum.

Aikijujitsu ("blending-forces style" *jujitsu*) instructor John Clodig, like many martial arts experts, holds black belts in more than one style. He believes advanced students need to practise different forms of martial arts to gain perspective. "You'll never understand your own system until you leave it," he says. (It's important to note this advice is intended for mature practitioners, not beginners who would be easily confused by flitting between several styles.)

Just as there are different martial arts, there are divergent management styles. Don't cling exclusively to the one you have adopted. Whether it may be *stratified* and *centralized* or *participatory* and *decentralized,* each management style has something to offer, and each has its strengths and limitations. Know them all, especially the range used within your organization. Then you're less likely to be blind-sided by a style you don't fully understand. You'll also be less threatened and better able to weave together different approaches in achieving common organizational goals. Just as important, different approaches will teach you about your own style.

It's also a good idea to keep abreast of the arts of management in other organizations, especially your competitors. Their progress may teach you about your own organization's patterns, weaknesses, strengths.

Become adept at all parts of a project: planning, budgeting, timing of milestones, decision-making, evaluation, writing, editing, marketing (internal or external), making presentations, and distribution. The more you really understand, the greater your control and the easier it is to delegate and monitor work or change direction quickly.

You can also improve your managing by referring to what you've learned in other arts. Just as Musashi, after his retirement, transferred his martial skills to *sumi-e* brush paintings, you can apply any other art you *truly* understand (athletics, public speaking, playing music, gardening) toward making you a better manager.

4. KNOW THE WAYS OF ALL PROFESSIONS

For the battle to be won, the Generals plot broad strategy, mid-level officers direct the fighting, and the soldiers are on the line. Many staff support the operation—the kitchen crew, the medical team, the record keepers, and so on.

Similarly, in any business, professionals must work together toward common aims. Each has an essential part in the functioning of the organization. You can help this along by taking a General's perspective. A General's perspective helps you understand the crucial role your department plays. Remember how much power you really have.

Unfortunately, because bright, otherwise capable managers too often have a narrow perspective, they neglect to notice their ability to influence the whole organization positively. Someone once said that a "professional" in an organization is someone who has a lot of power yet continually complains about how powerless he is.

This tongue-in-cheek description is often on the mark. I have heard all kinds of managers—in personnel, accounting, data processing, training, sales, safety, industrial engineering—grumble that they "have the answers, but no one listens." I also notice that a popular seminar topic in professional associations is "Getting Top Management Support."

Something's wrong. Yes, technical competence and interpersonal skills can make you adequate in your position, but they are not enough. If you wish to influence the *entire* organization, you must know the ways of all the parts, and those of other professions as well.

Many of us believe our professional expertise is the missing element that will solve organizational problems. But remember organizational professionals—including yourself?—are commonly stereotyped by others. Marketing staff are said to "shoot from the hip"; sales personnel promise customers anything to close the sale; and accounting professionals are tightly controlled, conservative, and detail conscious.

There may be *some* truth in these descriptions, but don't allow yourself to be pigeonholed. If you aspire to influence or to become upper-level management, think globally. Start by seeing the limitations of your own training. While all training systems claim they have no weaknesses and can handle all situations, in fact, each has problems it cannot readily defend against. So, whatever your background, broaden it. Become a "generalist."

- Expose yourself to professions far afield from yours. Take note of ones you don't really understand, then fill in the holes in your understanding. You're a data processing manager? Take classes or read books on salesmanship. A marketing specialist? Try personnel management.

  Also, meet with other professionals. Take breaks with them, have lunch together, and attend their professional meetings. This immersion approach, while helping you understand other systems, will also break down stereotypes (yours of them, theirs of you).

- When speaking to other professionals, use *their* language. All professions have a jargon; it's a way to recognize others in their field. Be able to speak of "cost benefits" to an accountant, of "loss control" to safety specialists, and of "gains in learning transfer" to a management development specialist. With language flexibility you can speak to different audiences.

- Begin to look at your own profession as if you were an outsider. Objectively assess the strengths and weaknesses of your training. Develop an understanding for different approaches (radical and conservative) within your field; look for the value and weaknesses of each.

- Rotate responsibilities or jobs. I know of several organizations that internally trade supervisors. This keeps the organization fresh and the staff alive, and provides perspective. Of course, these switches are not made haphazardly. First, input from the supervisor is solicited, and they work together closely for a smooth transition and orientation. ("Watch that problem that may come to a head.") Some Japanese companies are known for ably rotating managers—from engineering to marketing to personnel, and so on—as a key part of developing professional staff.

- Most importantly, search for similarities between your profession and others. If you look past the terminology, you will probably discover underlying principles you can apply to your own managerial skills.

One corporate officer in organizational development receives much praise from her colleagues for her advanced organizational ideas. She privately admits she hasn't been developing these ideas from scratch. She reads marketing journals and applies their latest findings to her own area.

With a widened perspective and a generalist's point of view, you'll recognize the interrelationships in your organization. You can boost organizational flexibility and strength by blending seemingly disparate professional approaches.

5. DISTINGUISH BETWEEN GAIN AND LOSS
   IN WORLDLY MATTERS

In order to make the right adjustments, the martial artist has to be able to see when he is winning, and when the tide is turning against him. This isn't as straightforward as it sounds. Too often, people become side-tracked, and don't remember their ultimate goal.

It's crucial that the martial artist not forget his true goals in the heat of battle. If you are playing for life, remember what is truly important. Seeking revenge or involving yourself in petty plotting are diversions if your true purpose is winning the battle, protecting others, or building a dynasty.

It is currently fashionable to criticize management for short-term profits. Books and consultants admonish managers to take a long-term perspective. Managers nod yes in principle, but in their hearts know that management theoreticians don't deal with the complex pressure they feel. The same managers who read the latest books or attend in-vogue seminars continue to be ruled by visions of immediate success.

Yet haven't you seen how an expedient decision to cut losses or reduce overhead has turned out to be costly after a short time? Sales had fallen far below worst-case predictions for a high-tech company. The managers looked for ways to thin out personnel and otherwise save costs. But one division manager went overboard; he had almost one hundred "unnecessary" telephone extension lines removed. Within seven months, the short-term crisis evened out and lines were reinstalled, at great additional cost. Unfortunately, the disruption to customer service and project management had longer-lasting effects than the added cost of installation.

If, like many managers, your own responsibilities aren't clear to you, how can you assess your performance? Solicit direction from your supervisor. If you can't get a clear signal from above, read company literature, follow the CEO's lead, consult with trusted peers. Don't let yourself get lost. Stay on track—remember what you should be doing. Like the martial artist, focus on results, not how many hours you've worked or how many meetings you've attended.

Once you know what's really expected of you, look at matters with short-term and long-term vision. Remember that a short-term loss may be turned into a large gain, and a short-term gain may lead to a major long-term loss.

The gain and loss maxim can be applied to the current trend in many companies of "profit centre" or charge-back accounting. In this framework, administrative departments are responsible for justifying their services. ("Yes, we can write you this software but we will charge the costs to your department's budget.") To departments accustomed to having captive markets within their own organization, this approach is often threatening at first. After all, under this scheme, the data processing department must compete with outside vendors for work in the warehouse. But properly implemented, charging back can improve service and organizational morale. ("Accounting is one of my *internal* clients.") The ensuing competition can enliven an organization and sharpen productivity. It can also clearly demonstrate whether a department is pulling its own weight. So a charge-back system can help clearly differentiate between internal profits and losses.

When you have losses, don't just accept them. Find ways of converting them into gains. "Breakdowns are not necessarily bad," contends black-belt information manager Mary Devlin. "It depends on what you do with them. If you're going to make things happen, you are also going to encounter more and more breakdowns. I try to remember to see these as signs of organizational movement, indicators of areas needing refinement, or opportunities to clean up previously submerged issues. And exposing people to this perspective can help them stay calmer and perform better."

6. DEVELOP INTUITIVE JUDGEMENT AND UNDERSTANDING FOR EVERYTHING

The martial arts emphasize the development of feeling. Practise the right way, learn all the techniques you can, work on them, be watchful, don't believe you know all the answers in advance. Then, maybe, the intuitive feeling will come. You will begin to understand.

Thought is too slow. Analysis can't defend you against attacks. When the glass falls off the table edge, there is no time to think about grasping for it. Think and it breaks. Notice and respond in the right way, and you'll catch it, moving so fast you won't believe your eyes.

Thought is predictable, out of tune with the motion of change. Too much thinking can make you vulnerable. In his technical treatise for advanced martial artists, *Precepts of the Martial Artist*, Walter Muryasz warns against thinking too much: "The more the conscious part of the opponent's mind is occupied, the easier it is to control. That is, the more thinking going on, the more openings occur. The more conditioned and unaware the mind is, the more easily it can be controlled. Thus, the martial artist's mind must become clear, aware, and open so as not to leave a place for his opponent to enter [and control it]."

When you use all of your resources, intellectual and intuitive, you'll have knowledge of *what* is going on combined with the feeling for *how* things are proceeding. A master of any art operates mostly on "scientific intuition." Knowledge plus real-life experience serves as the input, and the feel for "what's right to do here" is the product.

In living organizations, moments of opportunity or crisis can pop up at any time. A valued employee informs you she has been offered another job; should you let her leave or try to convince her to stay? An important customer is lukewarm about your new product idea; should you abandon this line or develop it further? There has been a reported rise in employee stress; should you investigate why or avoid opening a can of worms?

What do you do? If there is time to think, do so. But sometimes there isn't. Here's where you let intuitive feeling guide your actions. Use your intuition, and go with your impulse, *if you are calm*. If you have prepared yourself in advance for moments such as these, disciplined your mind, and learned from your experiences, your reactions will be your best ones.

Real life is complex. It is impossible to capture the whole picture through analysis. Just when you think you've got it, everything's changed. Nothing will sit still. People are unpredictable, certainly not the same from moment to moment. The market changes in peaks and valleys; no one knows what the economy will do or how seemingly distant events affect the organization. The past hints at the future, but is never actually repeated.

So what can you do?

- Develop your intuition in balance with your intellect.

- Orient your view to the entire system. Perceive the organization as a living, breathing organism.

- Look beyond the rules. New martial arts students are taught, "If he punches you this way, step back, always to his outside where it is safer." This gives the beginner the security of accomplishing an effective movement. But the sidestep doesn't always work. What if it carried you over a precipice? The beginner needs the rules, but the master *knows* the right time and *feels* when to forget the rules. He doesn't let rules or forms trap him. He knows when they don't apply, when to go beyond them, when to let them go.

   The rules are guidelines for typical situations; but remember that real life doesn't duplicate case book examples. Look beyond the forms and examples to find the underlying principles. With this in mind Bruce Lee described the martial art he developed, *jeet kune do*, as "the formless form."

   Which is more important, keeping up an image or being effective? If you choose the latter, remember that thoughts alone can serve as an initial guide, but too much thought without feeling and action only paralyses. Actions speak louder and prove more than words. The adept lets feelings guide his actions.

- Keep things as simple as possible. One general manager I know loves theoretical models. During the middle of a meeting or in a one-to-one discussion, he often rises abruptly to put up yet another graphic that "illustrates the problem." Don't make this mistake of falling in love with models for their own sake. Overdoing analysis removes you from reality. You've got the correct picture of the world, of the market, if only it would stay there. Some managers will disregard any glitch, data, or feedback that doesn't fit their favourite model or analysis. Clearly, this is dangerous.

- Stay connected. Don't manage from mental castles in the sky. Keep your feet on the ground, know your product and service, and sense organizational mood shifts.

7. PERCEIVE THOSE THINGS WHICH CANNOT BE SEEN

During one of his travels to Mongolia, aikido founder Morihei Ueshiba was threatened by an attacker with a gun, who was ready to fire at him from six feet away. Master Ueshiba disarmed the attacker. When asked how he did this, he replied, "a very long time elapses between the moment a man decides to pull the trigger and the moment he actually does so." Clearly, Ueshiba had developed the ability to anticipate an enemy's thoughts and actions.

Walter Muryasz has methods by which martial artists develop an ability to sense attack. He asks one blindfolded student to face a partner without a blindfold, just out of reaching distance. Muryasz instructs the blindfolded martial artist to relax, extend her perceptions, and tap her uniform when she senses her partner beginning to throw a punch or kick. Advanced students consistently sense an attack almost before it is launched.

You can also extend your perceptions by developing managerial antennae. Be on the lookout for the "invisible" factors that determine organizational reality:

- climate (atmosphere, mood)

- hidden agenda
  (Notice which stories and tasks others keep returning to.)

- intentions

- conflicts

- where change is resisted most
- where change is welcomed
- what *doesn't* get done
- who gets promoted, who doesn't
- what the competition is doing
  (Study your competition's strengths and weaknesses. Don't go into "battle" without adequate intelligence.)
- clients' reactions
  (Solicit feedback from customers who don't offer it on their own.)
- environmental factors that affect productivity and morale—colour, sound, use of space, lighting, temperature
- proximity of offices
  (Studies show that departments communicate less with each other the farther apart their offices are.)
- community perceptions of your business

These unseen factors form an early warning system that indicates organizational success or failure. Anyway, all your employees see the organizational web woven from these strands, so it's best you see them also.

Often, productivity trends aren't immediately indicated by statistical data. If you extend your antennae and stay in touch, you may be able to sense loss of momentum, incipient customer dissatisfaction, or the right time to act. By acting early, you'll save valuable time and catch problems before they take firm hold. You will also seize opportunities as they appear.

8. PAY ATTENTION EVEN TO TRIFLES

"From one comes many" goes an ancient *samurai* saying, meaning that little things add up until they spell victory or defeat. During the battle, will the sun be in our eyes or facing our opponent? What effect will the wind have on the contestants? Which small issues are indicators of an impending period of low morale? The trifles of today may become the troubles of tomorrow. Head them off while they are still small. Timing is the key to "trifle management."

In most organizations communication travels in a reverse pyramid. Grassroots rumours start at lower levels of an organization. So pay close attention to the morale and performance of entry-level personnel. Go to lunch or have coffee regularly with new staff. They'll see the organization with fresh eyes. Nurture clerical and hourly employees. They are important; people in these relatively low-paid, low-status positions probably have the most contact with your customers.

Pay attention to the effects of small things, like vacation schedules or when to call staff meetings. Learn to feel and use the natural forces in an organization—competition, attractions, jealousies, desire or resistance for change—toward increasing company strength.

9. DO NOTHING WHICH IS OF NO USE

Martial artists learn that efficient moves are strong and fast. The same is true in managing. Don't waste energy. Scampering around, looking busy, attending meetings, spending time on the phone are not the issue. Getting the job done is.

- Don't squander energy in needless worry or tension. Being relaxed means using only as much energy as needed to do the job. The world-class sprinter needs to be relaxed in the midst of the race, but tension is not the enemy. After all, he needs enough muscle tension to make the legs pump, swing his arms for momentum, and keep the upper body balanced over the hips. Misplaced tension however, helps no one. Clenching jaw muscles during the race only diverts energy from the task of finishing as quickly as possible.

  Make relaxation your ally. It releases otherwise bound energy, and helps you feel more powerful. Relaxation is a skill that develops with practice. A relaxed manager who can stay calm even when everything is in upheaval is more efficient. In dire circumstances, he is able to see opportunities unfold. He believes in himself, and so does his staff.

- Know what promotes organizational goals. There's no sense in working against the direction in which your organization is moving.

- Make only those decisions that need to be made. The only thing we have in this world is time; this is your most precious resource, so invest it wisely. Don't waste it on meaningless tasks.

In *Zen In The Martial Arts*, Joe Hyams suggests we must "conquer haste." Avoid pressuring yourself into making unnecessary or hasty decisions. Yes, there are deadlines that have to be met, but you can still control yourself and your time. Don't let yourself be *internally* hurried, even as you progress rapidly through your tasks.

- When under attack, there is a time to do nothing, if you are calm and alert. This attribute distinguishes an experienced martial artist from a beginner. There is a time to do nothing, when waiting and watching is the proper course of action. Move off the line of attack (on a straight punch, this may be just a few inches to the side), then punch or throw. The results will be disastrous if you try to do too much, grab that oncoming fist, cock back for a devastating hit, or try to force a throw. This will leave you vulnerable to even an unskilled counterattack.

Overactivity can harm a project just as surely as overwatering kills a plant. Being caught up in a frantic need for activity wastes your energy and power, and depletes the resources you will need when it is time to act decisively.

Ultimately, total position action is the bottom line. A positive attitude is a good start, but it is not enough by itself. An attitude just determines how you initially approach something.

Work doesn't have to diminish your quality of life. Just the opposite is true. Personal growth can easily be accomplished through your life's work. If you control yourself, use leverage to increase your organizational power, and act courageously, you can become a black belt manager.

THE BLACK-BELT MANAGER

Although small in stature, aikido master, Morehei Ueshiba could easily overcome multiple attackers or huge *sumo* wrestlers. He was reputedly never thrown or struck unawares. Rather than allowing his physical skills to wane with advanced age, he became more powerful and adept.

Karen Nish and Ron Swingen live different lives from Morehei Ueshiba's. But all three are black belts: Ueshiba in the martial arts, Nish and Swingen in the art of managing. Like the great master

Ueshiba, Karen and Ron's skills have evolved from individual aptitude and years of dedicated practice.

Karen Nish is a Divisional Operations Manager for Shearson Lehman Hutton/American Express brokerage firm. In a traditionally male-dominated industry, she is a small-framed woman with a warrior's spirit.

Ron Swingen is a senior manager at a large graphics firm, a leading high-technology company in computer aided engineering. Ron's career has been varied—teaching high school physics, sensitive work with IBM, engineering management at several large corporations. His work has consistently received high praise, but it's not what Ron seeks. He is determined to fulfil his own vision.

Although their arenas are on different battle grounds than Master Ueshiba's, Ron and Karen employ martial arts principles to multiply their business strength.

Black-belt managers may be of any age, size, or sex, and work in business, government, or nonprofit organizations. They practise their art at any level, often without being obvious. But black-belt managers share important characteristics with martial arts masters. They get the job done. They are powerful, undeterred by threat, and calm under pressure. In fact, they use their own fears to accomplish their goals. They act efficiently and take advantage of changing conditions. Others say they "make things happen" and "you can count on them." Most important, they control themselves first. Control and discipline are what gives a black-belt manager an unbreakable spirit.

How to Become a Black-Belt Manager: Techniques for Action

- Focus on the art and the science of managing. Start by studying the science. Become an expert at it.

- Dedicate yourself to training. Look for opportunities to sharpen your managerial skills. Practise what you have read, heard, and seen until new techniques become a part of you.

- Practise self-honesty. Know your true limitations. (There's no need to always admit these to others.)

- Trust your feelings. Listen and consider your inner voices.

- Develop your ability to train others. Through teaching, you can see what you truly know and where you are unsure.

- Rotate jobs. Look for projects that will broaden your base of experience and provide an opportunity to test what you know.

- Broaden your perspective. Be a generalist. Practise thinking like professionals with different training from yours.

- Develop your supervisory antennae. Learn to detect an organization's climate from the moment you enter the building.

- Don't wait for things to break. Intervene before they fail.

- Do nothing which is of no use. Don't squander energy.

- Focus on results. Help subordinates do the same.

CHAPTER TWO

Courage: Moving From Fear to High Performance

When we study the martial arts today, it is sometimes easy to forget that they grew out of violence and bloodshed. Martial arts masters were warriors, fighters who lived by the sword. Death and combat were part of their everyday reality.

It is said that in Japan, when the elite warriors came to the Zen monasteries to learn to overcome their fear of death, they became far more skilful warriors as a consequence. Although traditions and cultures have changed, I imagine that the taste of fear in men and women remains the same. Fear in all its many forms is still a component of daily life, and very much so in business "combat." It can be one of the biggest obstacles to high performance.

MASTERING FEAR

Tai chi chu'an master Andrew Lum says that fear comes from anticipation. In *Diary of the Way*, Mr. Lum is quoted as saying, "When you are in a dangerous situation you must never anticipate anything. What if this happens? What if that happens? Nothing has started and you are getting all prepared—for nothing! You must have a calm mind. Anticipation creates fear."

Mark out a path twelve inches wide on the floor and walk across it. No problem. Now lift this path two hundred feet in the air and walk across it. Your anticipation of falling may indeed make you fall. It is the same if two persons come to attack me. I do not say, "I have two persons in front of me; each one has two arms and two legs." In this way I have created eight problems. I have anticipated, and am drawing a negative conclusion that I have more of a chance of being hit.

Here is a typical situation. A person walks up to me with a mad face and automatically I assume he is mad at me. Maybe he is mad at someone else and maybe he is not mad at all. Perhaps this is his natural expression, and with his tone of voice he is an entirely different person. If, before he says anything, I react to his mad face, I have already worsened the situation. I have met him negatively and with a bad attitude. This is the point: if you anticipate an attacker will hit with his right hand, you are not alert to his kick. Never assume. You must be constantly aware.

The fear caused by anticipation creates doubt and lessons judgement. But fear is not necessarily bad. In some ways, fear can be looked upon as a good thing. If there is a little fear, one may be guided to the the point of not doing. If you cannot walk a tightrope, fear guides you to the point of not trying it. Fear is part of a message to give a little fair warning. Even fear has positive value.

Does fear ever get in the way of your performance? With the right attitude and training, you can make it an ally. Skilled managers are those who can harness the powers of heart and mind and find the courage to move toward the mission of their organization, particularly during trying times.

The martial artist must think, decide, and act under pressure. Walter Muryasz demonstrates how he defends himself in a frightening situation against four onrushing attackers. After one such demonstration, an onlooker approached the martial artist and asked why he wasn't afraid. "But I do feel fear," Mr. Muryasz replied, "I just don't let it paralyse me. In fact, the rush of feelings helps me move quickly." So he doesn't think of it as fear, but as energy which he channels into strong movement.

Managers can use this same method when confronted by decision-making stress. There may be many things to fear—budget shortfalls or cuts, negative reactions by subordinates to changes, or the exposure of past mistakes. But don't allow fears of what might happen stop you in your tracks.

Sometimes fear comes from having to act and not knowing the right thing to do. Like Mr. Muryasz, use fear. It can motivate you to work harder and to prepare better. Listen to it. The fear of negative consequences can make you rethink or delay a hasty decision. In either case, the effect of fear is positive, not paralysing.

THE POWER OF SELF CONTROL

Imagine this: a much larger person strongly grasps you by both wrists. Are you trapped? Not if you think like a martial artist. You'll know that no one can trap you but yourself. Your fingers are free, you can still wriggle them. You can move your shoulders up and down. You can shift your feet and bend your knees.

Only your wrists are trapped, not you. In fact, if you can train yourself just to relax your wrists, not to resist from where you are held, you can even bring your fingertips up to your head, just as if you were brushing your hair, while the attacker holds helplessly. Either you control yourself or you give up control. But no one else can trap you without your allowing it.

Martial arts adepts know they have to take charge of their own selves first because all power springs from self control. They monitor when they are feeling out of control. At those times, they actively resist the impulse to control others. The best tactic is to unbalance your opponent. A jujitsu expert knows he has to be close to the opponent's centre of gravity. He typically can't execute an effective throw at arm's length. The closer two bodies are—it's the Gravitational Law—the greater the force they can exert on each other.

In business, the closer you are *emotionally* to the "target" person or group, the greater your influence. A stranger may give me feedback about my style and, of course, I will listen. But although he stands a few feet away, he probably won't have as much influence with me as an old friend would, even if she resides three thousand miles away.

Proximity equals power. And who is the person you are closest to, the person you can influence most easily? Yourself. That's why martial artists and expert managers focus first on controlling themselves. A little effort here is most useful.

Perhaps you know someone who doesn't focus on controlling himself. Nothing seems to ever go right for him. He's always complaining, employees won't do what they are told, upper-level management just doesn't understand. And he is too cynical to solicit managerial help. ("What do they know?" or "That's easy for them to say, they don't have to deal with all the jokers I work with.") He believes you have to force people to work and change. In one way, he's right; employees don't work as productively for him as they do for other managers. The sad part is that he doesn't realize he is contributing to his own problems. He is out of control.

Everyone has a need for control. When people feel out of control of themselves, they attempt to control others, often in minor ways such as setting unnecessary dress codes, not allowing staff to place personal objects on desks, or insisting on rigid agenda-setting policies that prevent spontaneous meetings.

In trying to make others change, particularly outside one's sphere of influence—competitors, peers, legislators, other governments, supervisors, employees, spouse, children—many people are seldom effective, so they expend lots of effort without commensurate gain. And they feel helpless in the attempt. As psychologist Al Siebert said to me, the victim's theme song is "Wouldn't the world be a nicer place if everyone else would change?"

We all wish that everyone would change for our convenience, but they won't—at least not at our command, or when we want them to. Even if we could succeed in changing others—subordinates, co-workers, friends, boss, spouse, children, politicians—it would not ultimately help us to be in control of ourselves. Controlling others wastes energy, because it generates increased resistance. ("That's not in my job description," or "O.K., I'll do it your way, but you'll see it won't work.")

So what can you do to *influence* others? Decrease the distance and develop some emotional closeness with them. This doesn't mean you have to see them socially or be their friend. A work relationship is fine, but one in which you see and understand their point of view. Make real contact, bridge the gap, and your ability to exert influence will soar.

When you are working outside your sphere of influence or feel overextended, momentarily retreat into your place of power, your own environment, and watch calmly. Another moment of opportunity will surely present itself.

However, if you feel the desire to *control* others, watch out! It may be a signal that you feel out of control of yourself. Don't give in to these childish inner demands. Be honest with yourself. Of course, there are times when you're filled with apprehension and must still project a self-assured image. But don't lie to yourself. Be aware of your real worries and fears.

The failure to acknowledge stress is the biggest problem of the stressed manager, according to Cooper and Marshall in *Understanding Executive Stress.* Acknowledge your fears. And always admit what is obvious to others. People know when you are coming across as hesitant, so don't deny it. ("No problem, everything is under control.") If you do, you run the risk of losing credibilty by projecting mixed messages. Instead, turn your fears into strengths. *Before* being confronted, calmly admit your concerns. ("Yes, I am concerned about the staffing on this project.") This sets the stage for low-threat problem solving.

Most important of all, self control should protect you from ill-advised acts and words that once spoken can never be withdrawn. It's like getting kicked—the damage can last a long time. You may think it's forgotten, but those who suffer the impact of angry words can tell you otherwise.

A manager in a seminar told how she made this point to her son, after he had said something regrettable. First, she asked him to pick up a claw hammer and nail and meet her in the back yard. "Please drive the nail into that tree," she asked him. He did it. "Now, turn the hammer around and pull the nail out of the tree." He did it. "Now, take the hole out of the tree."

You can fill the hole with wood putty, but the tree will never be the same. Similarly, apologies may attempt to compensate for strong, angry words, but the relationship will probably be scarred. Haven't we all driven our share of holes into others' psyches and had holes—of various sizes—bored into ours? If you take the long-term view, if you would rather win the war than the battles, if you would prefer not to keep changing companies and cities to survive, control yourself before anger gets the better of you. Stop yourself before you say or do something you can't easily take back.

HOW TO BECOME A WARRIOR, NOT A WORRIER

In an ancient martial arts story, a student admitted to his teacher that he was frequently beset by worries and fears. "You may not be able to stop the birds from flying over your head," the master told him, "but you surely can prevent them from building a nest in your hair."

Maybe you can't prevent worries or fears from surfacing, but don't feed them by dwelling on them. When the fears are not a spur to positive action, just let them go and they'll die a natural death. Exhale slowly and deeply; it's a good way to let go of these cumbersome "birds."

Managers become tentative and less effective when they allow worry to consume them. They typically become rigid, unable to take risks, and incapable of profiting from opportunity. Staff and superiors will usually notice their self-doubt and question their leadership.

Rather than letting your worries back you into a corner, make them a spur to action. As physician Ken Paltrow tells people, "be a warrior, not a worrier." First attack those tasks you fear. Instead of being frozen by worrying about lack of job security, for instance, do something positive. Read a chapter from a professional career planning book; begin decision analysis by writing out the pros and cons of a career change; make an appointment with your boss to clarify your place in the organization; speak to a confidant to get your fears off your chest and get perspective.

Everyday management decisions may be as hard to face as major crises—whether to hire, fire, purchase, reward, ignore, plan, interrupt, review, or meet. (Pick any action verb you wish.) But decisions must be made and actions taken, without any guarantee that they will turn out to be the correct ones. Does decision fear sometimes grip you? There are some ways around it.

- Decide if the decision really needs to be made immediately. If not, wait.

- Analyse facts, then listen to your instincts. You can best pay attention to your instincts when relaxed, so use a favourite stress management technique to clear your mind and relax your body before making an important decision.

- When you have mixed feelings about a strategy, bring out these feelings for consideration. If you sense you have conflicting thoughts, but you can't bring them to the surface, take a walk and have a conversation with yourself to draw the feelings out. Carry a microcassette recorder and use it to talk out the decision. Just speaking aloud can clarify your thoughts—it may not even be necessary to listen to your recordings.

- Remember that you may not have to make this decision totally on your own. Invite input from all sides of the issue. If you're stuck, consult a trusted, respected mentor, supervisor, colleague, or consultant; or use them as a sounding board.

- Write out all sides of the issue. Then assign a weighted value to each advantage and disadvantage. Total the score of each side. You don't have to be bound by this device, but notice if your weighted decision corresponds to your overall feelings and thoughts.

- Bring two chairs face to face. Sit in one chair and argue for one side of the decision. Then switch chairs and argue for the other side. Continue until one side clearly dominates.

- Assign one side of the decision "heads," the other "tails." Flip a coin. Before looking at the coin, notice which side you hoped would come up. (It's not necessary to check the coin.)

Once you've made a decision, don't waste time worrying about its result. Your decisions—and those of the greatest, wisest managers—are sometimes wrong because of changing conditions, incomplete facts, or emotional involvement. Focus on making a high percentage of good decisions.

ATTITUDE CONTROL FOR A COURAGEOUS MIND

The right attitude is the foundation for a courageous mind. In 1981, I attended a martial arts retreat led by *aikido* master Mitsugi Saotome. After a dazzling display of self-defence tactics, Mr. Saotome laughingly dismissed his martial expertise. A winning attitude is really the key, he said. "*Before* the struggle, the victory is mine."

Ask any martial artist. Attitude makes the difference between whether a black belt's force "goes out" and breaks the brick or "pulls in" and damages the hand that delivers the blow.

Managers frequently talk about attitude; they may tell a subordinate he or she has a rotten one that must be changed. Sales superstars often point to attitude as the reason for their success. But what is attitude? Attitude means how you approach something. And a person's approach is crucial. Henry Ford probably said it best: "If you think you can or if you think you can't, you're probably right."

Aviation provides a useful analogy. A positive attitude means the nose of a plane is pointed up and it gains altitude; a negative one means the nose is pointed down. With a neutral attitude, the plane flies parallel to the ground, neither gaining nor losing height.

Your attitude doesn't do anything by itself; it just directs where and how you will put your effort. If you believe that "you can't teach an old dog new tricks" then you probably won't put in the time to learn something new. (By the way, animal trainers disagree with this adage.) Fortunately, many people refuse to believe the "old dog" maxim. For instance, Grandma Moses became an accomplished and successful artist at an age when most people would think of reasons they couldn't hold a brush.

Ultimately, everything begins as an attitude of one sort or another. This book was originally a thought in the mind of the author and publisher; even the pages as a mental concept of the paper-maker. Studies show that attitudes are important in everything from health to performance, to the ability to learn and adapt to change.

The next time you think of telling others they should change their attitudes, STOP. Be more specific—how should they do it? Also, do you provide a proper model? Are you able to change yours?

Managers set their organization's tone because they're in the centre of their department or company. Just as a pebble dropped in the middle of a lake spreads ripples throughout the water, a manager's attitude radiates directly to staff, and eventually through them to customers and the public. If you want good relations with internal or external clients, you must model this by treating your staff accordingly. In other words, managers determine the attitude message, and employees convey it to your customers.

Numerous management studies reveal the CEO's attitude is a prime determinant of employee morale. A manager participating in one of my seminars emphasized, "The executive must set the tone for the organization. If he is not enthusiastic about the goal, not honest on the job, and not positive, he will drag his staff down." In his excellent book *High Output Management*, Intel President Andrew Grove wrote of a depressed manager who, by trudging around the company with head hanging, spread depression throughout his department.

Understand the ripple effect of management attitude and you understand many sources of conflict and stress. It's like the child's game "Pass it on." I hit Peter and Peter hits Sara and Sara hits William and so on. Not only that, but Peter hits Sara harder than he got hit and Sara hits

William harder than she got hit. Unthinkingly, many adults still play this game. You feel pressured by your manager and you pass it on to subordinates. You bear the brunt of a customer's ire then unload that anger onto co-workers.

Not only is there a ripple effect at work, but in real life it also passes between work and home. Personal conflicts almost inevitably intrude on work. People beset with personal problems may not be disabled from doing their jobs, but they probably won't work in their top range of performance. One hopes the bottom of their range is still adequate. A manager who has unresolved personal problems will have an adverse effect on his staff, even though the underlying problems are "personal."

Fortunately, positive attitudes are just as contagious as negative ones. Learn to control your own attitude before others influence you negatively. In fact, a positive attitude can offset a generally negative environment. A forward-looking manager can help staff overcome the depression caused by a poor industry-wide economy. Rather than accentuating the problem, the manager can stimulate some solutions. ("How might we use these times to our advantage?") A deeply calm attitude will influence others' willingness to change. Once you know how to control your own attitude practically, you can teach this skill to your staff.

Confidence is also an attitude. Usually, when two swordsmen squared off to duel in a life-and-death encounter, they tried to intimidate each other. (The same "face-off" occurs before many boxing matches.) The winner of the match could frequently be decided before a sword had been drawn, let alone a blow struck. The winner was the artist who maintained his own composure in the face of the opponent's threat.

TECHNIQUES FOR ATTITUDE POWER

Attitude control, even for martial artists, requires effort. But this effort can pay large returns. Martial arts are a discipline. But discipline need not be gruelling; it means "to learn," not "to punish." Discipline is an organized method for increasing force and for solving problems, as well as a tool for self control. You will achieve self discipline by controlling yourself a bit at a time. Soon these moments of control will lengthen. Your power and effectiveness will grow.

Begin by practising single-mindedness. Martial arts training emphasizes single-mindedness, not splitting attention. Have you ever seen Japanese sword-fighting movies where one man single-handedly defeats scores of opponents? This is not just movie magic. In reality, even when several people attempt to launch a simultaneous attack, it is impossible for them to reach you at precisely the same moment. From the martial arts experts viewpoint, the attacks happen one at a time, albeit very quickly. The defender neutralized one attacker, then in the same flow (without pausing) moved to deal with the next threat.

Managers are sometimes beset by the "attack" of multiple problems. Do not carry problems. Deal with the most pressing, completely drop it, then move on to the next one.

Work cleanly. Psychologist Kurt Lewin's studies have shown that people tend to remember incompleted tasks. Worrying about these wastes time and energy. Find a way to complete tasks—or discard them.

The key is to be in the present, without distraction. The martial arts show instantly how single-minded your focus is. When sparring, there is only one thing in the universe—a fist, foot, or person coming at you. If your thoughts wander to anything else, you will surely get hurt.

In management, focus totally on whatever activity you're engaged in at that moment. Don't let yourself be distracted by irrelevant thoughts and worries. Let these go for the moment. Don't waste effort denying them or blocking them out.

For example, you may be delivering a presentation when you remember something you should have done earlier. There's nothing you can do about this during your talk, so don't allow this concern to distract you. All eyes are on you. This is an opportunity to influence many people. Can you discipline yourself to put aside irrelevant concerns? If you can develop this skill, during crucial times you'll be able to give your all.

Directly before the event—as a preparation—is the time to think about what might happen. Perhaps you have seen martial arts movies in which the protagonist mentally prepares himself the evening before the battle. He readies himself to live courageously or to die with honour, if that is what it comes to.

Martial artists also practise *kata*, an exercise that is a form of mental and physical rehearsal. Going through the motions of fighting imaginary opponents helps to prepare them for the real thing. They also enlist the imagination to program desired self-defence responses. They visualize: "What would happen if, as I walk to the corner, a large man leapt out of the shadows raining blows on my head? What would I do? Sidestep to the outside, use this briefcase I am carrying to block at the elbow . . ."

In the same way, managers can profitably rehearse their tasks. Before making a presentation or taking an interview, or anytime you will have to perform under pressure, perform a kata to prepare yourself. Practise the speech in your mind. Visualize yourself making that presentation decisively, or handling the difficult questions in the interview calmly and confidently.

Most of us have inappropriate attitudes and thoughts that we picked up during youth: I'm selfish, I can't draw a straight line, I'm small and afraid, I never could understand maths or technical things, or I have two left feet. These judgements, even if once true, are out of date—you're more experienced now and more capable. Use your conscious mind to undo negative fears and thoughts in your subconscious.

During the day, the conscious mind is dominant over the subconscious; this position reverses during sleep. Just before going to sleep, look into your own eyes in a mirror. This in itself is a powerful attitude change technique used by martial artists to take command of themselves. They also use the period before sleep, when the subconscious is coming to the fore, to focus on attitude control. Don't stare or focus on how your hair has grayed or thinned, or how your skin has aged. Just look deeply into your own eyes as you would a friend's. If this becomes uncomfortable and you nervously look away, you are probably uncomfortable with yourself at that moment. Don't give in to fear and discomfort! Look away, take a deep breath and look in your eyes again. When the tension builds up, look away, but keep returning to eye contact.

Next, say aloud a self-programming message: I am becoming more confident with the new system; I am finding ways to use uncontrollable changes to my advantage; I am letting go of fear and job insecurity. Be sure your tone of voice has the qualities that reinforce your message— strength, relaxation, and calmness. Then go to sleep. In a matter of a few weeks, your attitude will gradually but surely grow more positive.

Reflection is another useful attitude technique. Even in the midst of an attack, skilled martial artists take time, in the calm recesses of their minds, to reflect. What is the nature of the attack? Who is the most dangerous opponent? Where are the safe places to position myself?

Similarly, high-level managers take time, even when things are rapidly changing, to step back. Many black-belt managers spend a few minutes of each work day positively setting their attitude and mentally preparing for daily organizational concerns or ongoing work problems. Upon arriving at work, they go over what they are to accomplish that day and review their long-term goals. They may even talk their way through their program.

Whenever you need a mental boost, breathe, and silently talk to yourself. On inhaling, silently say to yourself in a calm tone of voice the first part of your suggestion—("I am becoming . . ."); finish the message while you exhale—(". . . more and more in control of myself each day."). A few repetitions work best. Your eyes may be either open or closed.

The power of this technique comes from combining breath and self-programming. It's also quite portable. You can use it to claim moments whenever you are waiting, on hold, standing in line, stopped at a traffic signal, in the shower, or even when driving to or from work.

Adaptability of attitude is another skill of the martial artist. In a strong grasp by an adversary, the best escape may be to yield flexibly to the point of attack. On the other hand, when the opponent is off balance, it's best to penetrate before he recovers, and get in that kick or throw.

Try this martial arts demonstration with someone. Stand to your partner's side. Ask her to stick her arm straight out in front, thumb up, and to "take the attitude" that her arm is made of *string*. Slowly and gently bend her arm. (One of your hands presses down on her elbow, the other up on her wrist.) Her arm will easily bend, like a limp dishcloth. Look at her expression and notice the demeanour.

Then ask her to shift attitudes and think of her arm as being made of *wood*. Her tension and facial expression will markedly change. Again, slowly bend her arm, *gradually and gently*, adding more force as needed. Wood is a material that resists, but will "break," suddenly bend in two, under a superior force.

Last, ask your partner to think of her arm as made of *steel*. To help her form a properly steel-like attitude, remind her that steel, in the building trades, is called an "elastic" material. Steel's strength comes from its giving a little under force, not being rigid. Again, attempt to bend her arm. If she can sustain a "steel-like" attitude, her arm will become almost unbendable. Watch her face. This is a useful technique to videotape. People can readily see the change in facial expression with each change of mental state.

You can shift your attitude better than you know. When the need arises, become string, steel, or wood. Are you trying to indicate to your superior that you are really giving in and will do it his way? Become string. Do you want to show a recalcitrant employee you mean business, that the line stops here? Become wood. Do you need to be friendly yet firm during important negotiations? Become steel. People will see your attitude in your face and treat you accordingly. Assuming the right attitude will reinforce what you want to communicate.

COURAGE TO RISK FAILURE AND SUCCESS

Martial artists emphasize that living courageously comes in part from conquering the fear of death. The *Hagakure*, an anonymous guide to warriorhood written in 1716, says it clearly:

> If a samurai practises introspection and self-criticism all the time and if, in addition, he is disposed to give his life where and when the need arises, he will be perfect in all the martial arts and lead an exemplary life.
> "The true spirit of the Way can be summarized as follows: it is fitting always to protect life as long as life is appropriate. It is by understanding the detachment of death that one can appreciate the value of life."

So the samurai stressed that warriors must look death squarely in the eye. Don't live dishonestly and don't live in fear. The only way to be truly alive and to live a full life is to accept the temporary nature of things.

Believing in life after death, the samurai thought a good death would result in a good rebirth—as a warrior again. A "good" death came from being true to your values so that your death counted for something. The samurai felt that one who chose life inappropriately, out of fear, became spiritually dead.

This definitely applies to managing. How? Some managers hang on at any cost—for a pension, biding time until retirement, or staying with an organization whose new direction is directly at odds with personal values. By doing so, they are choosing life inappropriately; self-respect lowers when fear rules. They usually appear pitiful and weak to others and to themselves. They don't help the organization or themselves, and are no longer alive professionally.

Courageous managers are willing to give up their organizational security at any time in order to say what needs to be considered, but might be momentarily unpopular. They will not be intimidated. They're not even afraid to recommend that their own positions be cut during a restructuring.

Clearly this is easier said than done. But courageous managers know there is no job security in the conventional sense. The only real job security is knowing inside yourself that you can get another position and will survive.

Like samurai, courageous managers are often blessed by good rebirths. Carol Maga is a true warrior and a black-belt manager. Her company asked her to head an organizational restructuring task force. She was the first to recommend that her position be eliminated. And it was.

People are impressed with this kind of courage, so I wasn't surprised that Carol was soon offered a more responsible managerial position within the same organization. In other cases, managers are reborn at new companies and find themselves stronger for the experience. Taking a voluntary demotion can also work out for the best sometimes. But accepting any demotion takes courage.

Samurai were told that if they wanted to come back from battle unharmed, they should give up thoughts of returning. The point is that the fear of death hinders the crucial survival skill of acting decisively. When you can no longer live with what you see, be willing to let your job "die." Don't throw away your career; just give up the fear of job loss and do what you have to do. Ironically, you may be all the more respected for your courage.

Leaving your position may not be the answer; just know that you have the option to do so. Many upper-level managers privately admit that they believe they could not procure an equally good position were their job to evaporate. This kind of insecurity can lead to increased political "rear-covering" and lowered creativity.

Shearson's Karen Nish believes courage separates the up-and-comers from the pack. "I supervise several managers who have the potential to do a higher level divisional job. But some are so afraid of failing, of getting out of their little comfort zone. What's going to happen if they take the job and it doesn't work out? How would they be able to go backwards? If they are successful, will they feel pressure to continue to rise? When I was promoted to divisional manager I had the same concerns. I asked myself, "Am I ready to change career paths and get out of the business if I fail?' "

Wise managers know there will be a price to be paid when they enter a new situation. Whether that price is increased responsibility, giving up the comfort of being immediately effective, taking time to learn new duties, renegotiating relationships with former peers or supervisors, or just plain risking failure, courage means entering the new battlefield with awareness in spite of the risks.

In any case, some degree of failure is not so terrible. It is said that Dr. An Wang, President of Wang Laboratories, applauds failure—to a point. He is quoted in a *Wall Street Journal* article, "If you try once and fail, I will know you have attempted something new. If you try twice the same way and fail, I will believe you are learning to correct any errors you made. If you try the same way three times and fail, I will fire you, because you haven't learned."

Like the children's game Warmer-Colder ("You're getting warmer— now you're hot—you've found it"), seeming failures can be the means for homing in on the winning answers. IBM purportedly has a saying, "the faster you fail, the quicker you will succeed." Similarly, the bestseller *In Search of Excellence* exhorted managers to "Ready-Fire-Aim." In other words, you have to try something and adjust until you're on target.

Just as you can feel generally healthy yet have a sore throat, you can become comfortable with outer "failure." Remember that today's failure may actually be the groundwork for tomorrow's success. If you try to learn to ski you'll see all beginners fall frequently. It's embarrassing and perhaps painful. But learning to ski—or mastering anything new—means getting through this initial phase of discomfort. ("Am I making the right decisions?" "Do I look foolish?" "Should I have accepted this position?")

In 1980, I attended a week-long martial arts seminar. The instructors were excellent. I had been a teaching black belt for a few years and was puffed up with youthful pride. But I was disappointed to discover that not only was I unable to do what the instructor was demonstrating—I expected that—but I could not even understand his technique well enough to work on it. I was depressed for two days. A part of me tried to deny my discomfort. ("Well, after all this is different. The people here are trained to attack differently," and so on.) But I wasn't progressing and I knew it.

It took me a few days to admit that I was uncomfortable. My pride was shaken; I was a beginner again, but this was all right. I could accept it and be comfortable underneath, even though I was outwardly struggling and uncomfortable. "Becoming comfortable with discomfort" improved my outlook. More importantly, I spent the remaining four days of the conference soaking up knowledge and techniques that have stayed with me to this day.

THE COURAGE TO BE INVISIBLE

There is a practical reason martial arts masters don't brag about their skills. If you don't broadcast ("I can break three boards with one kick"), the opponent is not forewarned. "Invisible" actions are difficult to counter or resist.

In the same way, invisible managers can accomplish more. This means not giving in to the craving for recognition. Most people have this need, but it can get in the way.

Sometimes Shearson's Karen Nish is called upon to change procedures with branch managers she doesn't supervise. Ordering won't work. Karen's approach is to present a new operations picture in a way the branch manager can accept. Sometimes, she will later hear the manager talking about the wonderful procedure "he" instituted. Part of Karen, of course, wants to say, "Wait! Remember this was my idea." But she doesn't. By controlling her desire for recognition, she preserves rapport with her colleagues and insures effectiveness for the future.

Ironically, not trying to gain recognition means you often win the greater prestige of being seen as a doer. Seeking approval usually doesn't pay off anyway because trying too hard to impress others looks weak; it can also divert you from taking difficult—and necessary—actions. Just as important, a "look-what-I-just-accomplished" posture can impede team spirit. Instead, if you give up power you may gain power.

In *Further Up the Organization*, Robert Townsend quotes Lao Tsu:

"As for the best leaders, the people do not notice their existence. The next best, the people honour and praise. The next, the people fear; and the next, the people hate. When the best leader's work is done, the people say, 'We did this ourselves.' "

According to Steve Christie, Executive Director of the International Communications Association, managing a large association is a "back-of-the-scenes kind of job. The directors and officers are the outward face of the association. . . . The director is really the guiding force behind it and tries to make sure that the volunteers, board members, and staff proceed on the right course, are at the right place at the right time, saying the right thing."

Sharing the credit and the responsibility will eventually pay off in a more vigorous organization. Christie further says, "If people really sense the job they're doing is needed and their efforts are crucial to an activity, you get much more response and activity from them than if you just assign some silly nonsensical type of job."

THE COURAGE TO GIVE IT AWAY

The black-belt manager is confident enough of his abilities to give away many of his tasks. Delegation of authority should not be a difficult issue; in fact, dividing and allocating tasks seems one of the easier jobs managers must perform. But it doesn't work out this way.

Even though they usually have the best intentions, some managers do more grumbling than delegating. That is, they mean to spread the workload among subordinates, but typically wind up doing most of it themselves. Not that they don't do good work. It's just that they are limited in what they can accomplish, so they don't get everything done—and they wind up with employee morale problems as well. Why don't these managers delegate work better?

Delegation is an issue of fear. First it can be the fear of things not being done "the right way." When you delegate a task, people will not do it the way you would. They may do it better, they may do it worse, but they will do it differently. Underlying an "if-you-want-it-done-right-do-it-yourself" attitude can be discomfort with change or a mistrust of your staff.

Concern with being shown up can be another underlying fear. What if I give you this project and you do it better than I could? You may become more acclaimed than I, or you'll find that I don't know all the answers.

Delegation fear number three: If I give up what I do best, what will I do then? Probably something new and uncomfortable (that may force me to change, adapt, and grow).

If you have problems delegating, it's essential to be honest about your own motivations. Look beyond surface mistrusts and discomfort to the deeper fears that grow best in the dark. Confront them and weed them out if they're depriving you of the ability to delegates. Here are some tips for developing the courage to delegate:

- Choose the way of power, not the way of fear. When deciding between delegating a familiar task and one you don't know well, delegate what you know. By delegating the familiar, you can give subordinates expert advice, monitor their work, and learn new skills yourself. If you delegate unfamiliar tasks, it becomes the blind leading the blind.

- Think of delegating as helping people grow—both your subordinates and you. Expert managers usually report that developing their people is a major management benefit. If you don't trust your staff enough to delegate, better not to be managing them. In these competitive times, it's like leading an uncertain army into batttle. Change something. Strengthen your staff or replace them. Or change jobs.

- Give up the desire to be indispensable. No one truly is. Extra work and lowered staff morale are the price of seeming irreplaceable.

THE COURAGE TO CREATE

In *The Zen Way To The Martial Arts*, Taisen Deshimaru writes, "Life's problems are different for each of us and each of us needs a different way of solving them. Therefore, each of us has to create his own method. If you imitate, you'll be wrong. You have to create yourself."

Beginning martial artists generally don't create. They are more than happy to mimic their instructor's moves. They practise defensive reactions to specific attacks from set angles—a straight thrust to the stomach, a round kick to the ear, a cross-hand grab. This is not yet true martial artistry. In real life, situations are uncontrolled and attacks are not made according to the classic models. The straight stomach punch may veer into a hook, the round kick can slip down to the neck, or the grab be combined with an elbow strike. High-level skill entails developing new movements as called for by the nature of the attack and the layout of the room, actually changing the defence in mid-air to something that may never have been done before.

Most managers say creativity is important, but don't practise it. They allow fear to block them. Obviously, in the middle of an attack or crisis, it can be frightening to create a technique or to try something new that may not work. You can lose your life or limb. But in reality, you may encounter an attack for which you know no defence. Pretending this attack is similar to one you've experienced may not protect you. If you can't create a solution, you will die just the same.

Sometimes sticking with the "tried and true" has its price. You will lose your life, but more slowly, wearing down as you absorb kicks you haven't quite parried. It's not the path I choose to follow.

Creating means finding a different way to do something. One software development manager described his role of developing technology as "creating reality." You have to be unwilling to settle too quickly, to get too comfortable, or always to agree with the status quo. This can be risky, especially if you're not independent by nature. But keep in mind what one wise manager said: "If two people in the same organization always agree, one of them is unnecessary." If you don't create, you may be the one to go.

Creativity, of course, is not an excuse for blind rebelliousness, just as honesty is not a rationale for insensitivity. Someone who disagrees for disagreement's sake is not being creative. Automatic response is actually cloaking the fear of not being heard, or of being seen as weak or passive.

Mentor Graphics senior manager Ron Swingen says, "I think creativity comes once I've chosen to do something different. The rebel aspect might get me on the course. But once I'm there, my God, now what am I going to do? I've pushed off or I've opted out, but that was only a beginning. Now, from here on, I have to do something—I've got to be able to swim—or learn fast."

The courage to create means being willing to risk ostracism or rejection; it means not accepting any problem as unsolvable and never being satisfied with mediocre results.

The second creativity-killing fear is that of looking foolish. Ask anyone who creates for a living—artist, software developer, or organizational designer—they'll tell you, "I do have many good ideas. But what you don't see are the countless terrible ones I throw away."

Creating means being willing to fail. Ultimately, volume is the key to developing a few good ideas: come up with many ideas, sort them out, then focus on the ones with promise. Sometimes the terrible ideas are actually steps on the way toward the great ones.

Don't be waylaid by the temptation to find an easy answer, one that has been successful for others and will involve no risk. ("IBM does it this way—you should too." "Have a difficult employee? Just send him to our seminar; we'll straighten him out." "Everyone needs to read this book and manage exactly like the authors say.") But these solutions are unlikely to help unless they are creatively adapted to your situation.

Just like self-defence skills, the courage to create comes ultimately from practise in creating. But creating without a strong understanding of the fundamentals usually leads to impractical or weak actions. It takes time and experience to learn how to test realistically your new techniques or products. Change is possible; a manager may markedly increase his or her effectiveness—but not effortlessly, not entirely smoothly, and only with persistence.

So observe critically, listen, and read for ideas. Then ask which approach would work in your situation. Will participative management techniques really apply to your organizational culture? Can you adapt them into something workable?

For instance, workers may rebel if you try to copy the Japanese practice of starting the work day by formally reciting the company motto. But you can adapt the underlying principle by assembling your people together in the morning for a few minutes to discuss the purpose of this day's work or to positively set their attitude and plan of action. In this regard, United Parcel Service drivers meet for a few minutes at the beginning of their work shift to discuss potential safety hazards and other concerns; these meetings have helped to greatly reduce accidents. Or you can offer pre-work physical stretching exercises for those who are interested.

Have the courage to find your own solutions. Here are some creativity tips:

- Think of yourself as an "artist" manager, creating your organization and career. Where should your organization be reshaped? What tools do you have to do this? Think of your organizational culture, and ask what limitations go with working in this "medium."

• Practise simple relaxation techniques each day. Relaxing stimulates creativity.

• Develop brainstorming "muscles." Create first, and evaluate second. By yourself and in groups, list—without criticizing—possible solutions to problems. Practise turning off critical thinking while brainstorming.

• Write down six qualities that are unique to your organization, that make it different from others in the field. (For example, there are many long-term employees; staff is highly family-oriented or enthusiastic about sports; or there are new managers.) Then think of ways that employee programs can be adapted to these qualities.

• Meditate as martial artists do to tune in to your intuition. Before making any big decision, STOP! Take some time alone, relax, and listen to your inner voice. Do you have any inclinations toward or against the pending decision? Whether you choose to follow your inner hunch or disregard it, watch the results of the decision. How accurate are your inner feelings? How well do you listen to yourself? At first this voice will speak faintly; you have to learn how to listen.

• Read a practical book on creativity. (See Roger von Oech's *A Whack on the Side of the Head* or George Prince's *The Practice of Creativity*.) Select one technique out of those suggested and practise it three times each week.

• Using outside hobbies or skills as metaphors, think of other ways to develop your management art and creativity. How can gardening principles be applied to helping *people* grow? Can you use skiing methods to help you stay on balance in front of organizational "moguls?" Can golf concentration techniques help you perform when you are about to close a deal?

The martial arts teach that true power can only spring from within. Inspect yourself as you would a weapon and notice your flaws and virtues. Ultimately only you can correct your weaknesses and polish your strengths.

You will have the greatest effect if you stay within your sphere of influence. Harness the energy of a positive attitude and the energy from your commitment to advance your professional strength and that of your organization.

Developing Courage: Techniques for Action

- Practise something out of your range of comfort. Note your discomfort, but don't give up. This new activity can be simple—eating or playing a sport with your opposite hand, or changing the order in which you dress—or more complex—learning to program a computer, or to speak before a large group.

- Take reasonable risks. Be willing to stand by your opinions, but be equally able to admit when you have steered far off course. Have the courage to look awkward in public. Try new things and smile at yourself if you feel slightly foolish. Be willing to say, "I don't understand."

- Monitor yourself closely when you are afraid, threatened, or angry. Catch yourself before you lose control of what you say or do.

- Mentally consider giving up job security; the fear of losing your job may have ruined your ability to take reasonable risks.

- Practise attitude control every day, even when things go smoothly.

- Spread recognition. Silently congratulate yourself on the job you are doing, even when others get credit. Notice if this approach results in more vigorous staff commitment and efforts.

- Think differently; try something new. Apply the unknown to what you know. Think critically; act creatively.

CHAPTER THREE

Using Leverage to Magnify Your Strength

Don Angier, master of *shidare yanagi-ryu*, performs an impressive demonstration. Angier asks a large black belt to rush him. Although he is a man of small stature, Angier easily repels the much larger attacker with one small, easy punch. There's no wind-up, and he apparently exerts no effort.

How does he do this? Angier says, "You don't need to pull back your fist to punch forward. And don't tense up unnecessarily. Just relax and let your power flow into your opponent." This is the principle of leverage: using minimal force for maximum gain.

A jujitsu practitioner does not have to be big to get the job done. He knows that by an understanding of leverage, a little force can produce impressive results. Managers can also employ this principle.

Black-belt managers should use both mental and physical leverage, and the first step is to establish presence. Rightly or not, others judge your confidence and competence by how balanced, relaxed, and calm you appear. Most powerful managers have a strong presence or charisma. They exude confidence, move with power and grace, and are rarely pushed, always calm and balanced.

How you deal with the physical world is a test. If you don't know how to use your body efficiently to lift a chair or open a heavy door, how do you expect to move an organization? Size or physical strength is not the issue. It's knowing how to use your energy, mentally and physically, that gives you a strong presence. There are tangible martial arts methods to help you develop a strong presence.

DEVELOPING PHYSICAL LEVERAGE

Martial arts adepts know that a strong body engenders a clear mind. Like beginning martial artists, learn how to control your balance, posture, and breathing.

Moving with Balance

Balance is an interesting word. It connects both a mental and physical state. A weak person may be said to be a pushover, easily swayed, or unstable. Think of the implications of "mentally unbalanced."

In a martial arts demonstration of the centre of gravity, someone lies on his back and an *obi* (sash) is slipped underneath him just below the navel. Two people take each end of the belt and lift him by it. He balances perfectly, suspended. When the obi is positioned a little off centre he no longer balances. Extra strength is needed to control his weight.

A small shift at the centre of gravity results in a major effect on your balance. This is an important principle for physical well-being. Without physical balance, it is difficult to achieve relaxation or to maintain energy reserves. The more balanced you are, the more muscle tension you need to keep from falling over. On the other hand, being balanced takes less energy; it employs gravity and natural posture to keep you upright. So the more balanced you are, the lower your baseline tension level and the more energy you'll have to direct toward your work. Martial artists call this life energy *ki* (Japanese and Korean) or *chi* (Chinese), as in the *ki* in *hapkido* or aikido, or the *chi* in tai chi ch'uan.

The easiest way to develop good balance is through the *hara*, your centre of gravity. Located between your hips in your lower abdomen, the hara literally means "life centre." Contact the hara by mentally relaxing your lower abdomen, your inner core. When you sit or stand, feel the pull of gravity, the weight of your upper body falling through your lower abdomen, down through your legs and into the ground. When angry or upset, let your weight settle through the hara. Feel the hara open as if empty. Don't tighten up your lower abdomen; this will make you feel uptight. Instead, let it relax.

Also, feel your weight fall through an open hara as you perform normal tasks. Let this feeling be in the background, in the same way that you can speak in a meeting and still read others' reactions without being distracted from your talk.

Motion coming from the centre of gravity is always balanced and more powerful. Feel any motion—walking, shaking hands, writing—as generated from the hara, in the same way a motor drives a machine's extensor arms and legs. When you point your fingers, feel them being lifted by the hips, like a winch smoothly hoisting a bar. This economy of motion will leave you with more available energy. In addition, you will feel and appear much calmer. Michel Random wrote, in *The Martial Arts*, "Concentration on the *hara* creates a stable and serene strength."

Posture Power

All martial arts emphasize taking appropriate stances and postures. Your posture has many effects on your ability to control yourself and apply your physical and mental power to the world around you. One martial artist put it this way: "Whenever one of those guys sizes me up, thinking he can intimidate me, I *move*. I don't know quite how to say it, but I can control the situation, pretty much get what I want, by how I stand."

Leverage means realizing a sizeable return from expending a small amount of effort. Posture control provides a sizeable return from a small effort. By controlling your posture, you direct your power more efficiently, and greater mastery over yourself.

Don't think of posture as a static position. In fact, posture is an ever-changing state, a sort of frame-by-frame motion picture that's more than just sitting upright or standing straight. Proper posture had many wide-ranging effects.

• Mental alertness. Try this. Exaggerate a slumped position. (It doesn't matter if you collapse back into a chair, slump over a desk, or stand with shoulders well-rounded.) Notice how alert you are. Is it easier or more difficult to daydream? Most people report they become far less alert when slumping.

Breathing is shallower because the weight of the upper body collapses onto the diaphragm, the muscle responsible for deep breathing. You can feel this tension in the diaphragm by placing your hands just below the rib cage as you slump.

Shallow breathing reduces the oxygen supply to the cells. The first organ affected by oxygen deprivation is the brain. So if you slump while trying to make an important decision or working out the nuances of a vital business relationship, your brain may be only working at half power. Your mind drifts and you aren't able to concentrate.

When you want to feel more alert or you need your full mental power before making important decisions, align your posture and take a few deep breaths. This clears the mind and often allows you to consider other options that you couldn't previously see with your brain in an oxygen-deprived state.

- Energy/vitality level. Try slumping again, but this time notice your level of physical energy. Is it higher, lower, or the same as a few minutes ago?

  Cells create energy through a process called oxidation; less oxygen means less energy created. Posture control is a relatively simple method of raising your energy level.

- Efficiency. Posture control means moving efficiently, in balance and with a minimum of wasted motion. Reducing wasted motion conserves your energy and prevents strains and pulled muscles that result from overuse or overextension. Properly positioning yourself, with good posture, near your work and telephone, will eliminate stretching and overextension that can exhaust you by degrees.

- Communication. Your posture communicates non-verbal cues to other people and to yourself. For example, we see depressed or unconfident people as slumped, and rigid or anxious people as having stiff spines.

What posture do you associate with a powerful martial artist? His back is probably straight and strong without being rigid. Think of the posture of the most powerful managers you know. How many of them are slumped or overly tight? Most I've met convey a sense of presence. They seem relaxed, strong, and in control. How much of their demeanor do we read from their posture? Posture control enhances your presence, so that you actually seem bigger and more powerful.

Besides communicating to others, your posture also affects how you feel. If you feel hopeless or trapped with no way out, check your posture. You may be slumping, which makes you less alert mentally, and less able to do something to rescue yourself. Adopting the right posture puts you in the action mode that can lead to effective performance. Brainstorming and decision-making will go markedly better when you adopt an alert posture.

Hindrances to Good Posture

With all these benefits—mental alertness, increased energy, greater physical efficiency, and the ability to communicate a positive presence—why don't all people adopt strong, effective posture? They may have problems that prevent good posture:

- Poor self-image shows itself in weak, collapsed posture.
- Poor physical conditioning may be reflected by stiffness or rounded shoulders.
- Poor movement habits, such as bending with locked knees, or standing at an uncomfortable distance when moving objects, can make people physically awkward (and injury prone).
- Past injuries, such as a broken back, may make a relaxed, strong posture difficult to maintain.
- Clothing can shift a person's weight or restrict natural, relaxed movement. Examples are high heels and tight waistbands, jackets, skirts, or pants.

Elements of Posture

For the first two years I studied *kenjutsu*, my sword instructor had me do only one movement. He tested my postural strength with small pushes from different directions and observed closely. He insisted that the correct posture would be a building block to more advanced, powerful movements. As boring as this study was, he was right. My sense of power increased until it spilled over into my other movements in the unarmed arts.

Posture can be broken down into eight elements that describe how the joints align. Each element deserves exploration simply because it affects all the others.

1. Ankles and feet. Weight should fall through the arches, not over the heels. Walking on your heels, as many people do, reduces physical balance and usable strength. This can lead to feelings of being weak, intimidated, and easily controlled. Check the wear patterns on your shoes. Do the corners of the heels wear faster than the mid-sole? If so, consider a small adjustment. Lean forward slightly until your weight falls through the arches. Standing more upright may feel like falling forward, *by comparison* to your old posture. If you do feel you're falling, ask a friend to push you forward *lightly*. If your posture is right, you will know it—your balance will be strong.

Here's a good way to spot your weight over your arches. Lift your heels off the ground by standing on your toes and the balls of your feet. Then, bending the knees, let your feet come down flat. Bring your weight straight down; make sure not to drift back to your heels. This exercise usually places weight correctly.

You can even balance over the arches when wearing high heels. With these shoes you are, in effect, perpetually walking on a downhill slope. You can be balanced going downhill, but not by walking as on level ground. Adjust your balance accordingly, until your weight falls over the arches. Don't allow your shoes to undermine your balance.

On the other hand, if you walk by falling onto your toes, correct your balance by adjusting *back* to the arches. Again, check shoe wear to tell if you walk on your toes. Does the front of the sole wear faster than the heels? Those who walk on their toes usually find themselves stumbling frequently.

2. Knees. Knees are physiological shock absorbers. Locking them makes them less able to absorb shock before it reaches the upper body. If someone walks or jumps with locked knees, the impact passes on to the head. Knees are also important to body balance. Standing or walking with locked knees is like being on stilts.

Moreover, tension in the knees, as in any joint, spreads upward. So locked knees result in lower back tension. Try standing and placing your hands on your lower back muscles. As you slowly lock your knees, you'll feel the lower back tighten.

For best balance, control, and relaxation, put a little spring in your knees, and avoid standing or walking with knees locked. When waiting in line, practise unlocking by rhythmically, slowly, and imperceptibly shifting your weight from foot to foot, with your knees slightly bent.

3. Hips. Too much hip cant (being swayback) adds to lower back tension. When standing, slightly tuck the hips under you, as if you were just beginning to sit down.

4. Spine. The shape of the spine affects your body balance. Perhaps more importantly, it strongly influences your emotional state.

There are three basic spinal shapes—C-shaped (slumped), I-shaped (rigid), and S-shaped (natural). If you have ever looked at a skeleton or anatomy chart, you can probably visualize the natural, slightly flattened S-curve of the spine.

As mentioned above, a slumping, C-shaped spine reduces oxygen intake, thus lowering mental alertness and physical energy. Slumping is not, as some people believe, a relaxed posture. It creates tension in other joints such as the upper back and neck. To check this, place your hands on the muscles along the neck, then gradually slump in your chair. Muscular tension in the neck increases.

But martial artists believe anything can be turned to their advantage. There is a time when slumping is useful. When your mind is racing and you can't shut it off—"What am I going to do about that contract? Will the merger go through? Should I start looking for another position?"— slumping slows things down temporarily. Just a little such collapsing decreases mental alertness and slows thought, so be careful not to go overboard. Action is the bottom line. Slow things down only to the point that they are manageable. Then, pull yourself into an S-shaped posture, so that you are better able to plan something that will change things for the better. Sit up naturally. Lean forward, push your hips back so they are supported by the chair. Take a deep breath and relax, without collapsing. You'll be more alert and ready for crucial decisions.

With I-shaped posture, weight falls over the heels, and deep breathing is difficult. A rigid, inflexible body loses the ability to absorb the impact of walking and other normal movements. The result is tension, especially in the neck and shoulders. In the same way that a heavy plank standing on end can be easily toppled, such rigidity makes you a pushover for any outside force.

In general, a natural S-shaped posture is the most relaxed and the best for body balance; it also promotes clear thinking and strong interpersonal communication. To bring yourself to S-shaped posture while sitting, reach behind your chair and grasp one wrist with the opposite hand. You can't easily slump in this position. This technique is suitable for staff meetings. Not only can you breathe deeply, you will convey confidence as well.

If you get fatigued when sitting for long periods, support your lower back in a nonslumped position with a small throw pillow. Not only will the pillow reduce back pain and fatigue, it will also help you maintain an emotionally and mentally powerful position.

5. Neck and head. The neck is a column which supports the head (it weighs about the same as a bowling ball). Head position has great influence on balance and power.

In martial combat, grabbing the front of an opponent's hair may pull some out and anger him, but won't efficiently affect his balance. Pulling the hair on the back of the skull has a similar result. But you can easily take him off balance by lightly grabbing his hair at the crown.

For maximum balance and strength, as well as minimum neck tension, the crown should be the highest part of the head. This works both in walking and sitting. To get this feeling, pull your hair up at the crown. (If you don't have enough hair on the crown, pretend you do.) Place your hands on the neck muscles while you slowly move your head up and down. Most people find the crown-high position causes the least tension. Relax while keeping this crown-high position. In other words, stand proud and tall. Walk with your head held high, but don't put your nose in the air.

6. Shoulders. Keep the shoulders relaxed and down. Don't hold them up. Carrying the shoulders high has several negative effects. It makes deep breathing very difficult. (Try raising your shoulders and notice what happens to your breathing.) It increases neck/head tension. It raises your centre of gravity and tends to make the knees lock. (Try it. Raise your shoulders while standing. Watch what happens to your knees.)

When people get angry, their shoulders often rise. In turn, this makes them feel and appear out of control. Anger can be powerful when it signals to others that you are serious and expect immediate action. But don't let anger make you lose control. When you are angry, you can still remain relaxed by letting your shoulders stay down. Just exhale and drop them if they begin to inch up.

7. Elbows. When your arms hang to your side, they have a natural bow. It's unnatural to lock them. When you overstraighten your elbow, your arm becomes a lever against yourself, slightly raising the shoulders. The elbow is also more vulnerable to injury in this position. Typically, people lock their elbows when they overreach.

8. Hands. How you use your fingers makes a big difference in your strength and physical balance. A jujitsu grasp emphasizes the strength in the thumb and last two fingers (the ring and little fingers). These fingers are connected to long, strong muscles that indirectly connect to the centre of gravity in the hips. Use your entire hand, but grab and hold by emphasizing these fingers.

Controlling these eight postural elements may seem like a tall order. But because everything is connected, a small effort at shaping the spine will improve your control over all the other elements.

Breathing: Stoking the Inner Fire

Breathing influences your ki or energy level and is the gateway to subconscious mastery. Because every martial art focuses on developing both the body and the mind, breath control is an important part of martial arts training.

Breathing is the only essential bodily function that can be controlled consciously and unconsciously. When your attention is not on your breathing, you breath just the same. Focus on it consciously, and you can adjust your breath. In order to strengthen your power, practise one of these breath-control techniques.

- Take natural, full breaths. Always inhale through the nose. First fill your hips, then let the rib cage expand, finally fill into the chest below the shoulders, so the collarbone rises.

  Exhale in the reverse order. As air leaves, let the shoulders lower, the rib cage deflate, and finally the abdomen contract. If you are breathing naturally, your shoulders will actually rise and fall slightly. This is a good exercise to do before sleep; eventually it becomes part of your normal unconscious breathing pattern.

- Exhale strongly when you feel disheartened or intimidated. Have you ever seen samurai movies in which two swordsmen duel? Both wait and watch. Suddenly, there is a flurry of powerful action; only the victor walks away. In fighting of this sort, skilled swordsmen watch their opponent's breathing. They know that actions taken while inhaling are weaker and less positive. When they feel the opponent inhale, they attack. So to limit their vulnerability, they practise a "fighting breath"—long exhalations with imperceptibly quick, yet full inhalations.

  During crucial times, when you feel under the gun, control your breathing and focus on exhaling. Make your exhalations long and even. Breathe in normally. Naturally, if you exhale fully, a partial vacuum is formed in your torso which in turn draws air in. Breathing this way will help you to overcome fear and to act with all your strength.

- Use sound to monitor your breath. When you exhale, make a "huuuh" sound from deep in your abdomen (not shallowly forced from your throat). Is the sound you make short and choppy or long, smooth, and even? Practise making the sound of your breathing long, smooth, and even.

- Raise your energy level with *misogi* (deep cleansing breath). When you exhale, make sure to expel all the air out from your diaphragm, ribs, and between your shoulders. On inhaling, fill your entire body cavity, especially the hara, ribs, and shoulders.

- Breathe to reduce physical or emotional pain. Tae kwon do practitioners learn to do this when they receive a solid blow during sparring. Place the tip of your tongue on the roof of your mouth, at the front of the palate. Exhale sharply from the abdomen. As the pain subsides, gradually slow down your breathing and continue to let it emanate from the lower abdomen.

Movement Using Physical Leverage

If you wish to increase your understanding of leverage, use your body during the day to explore the principle. Practise how to open a heavy door with minimal effort. Discover precisely where to push and how to get maximum strength from your body. (Hints: Touch the door with your little finger or the edge of your hands and sidestep to push, rather than fall into it.)

Some other ways to increase physical leverage are these:

- Keep your head, shoulders, and knees pointed in the same direction. Martial artists know this is generally the strongest body position when you are delivering the blow or executing the throw.

  If you want your presence to be strongly felt, don't swivel your head to talk. Instead, turn completely. You can even move your chair around to face the other person. This may seem like some effort, but the returns are great. Conversely, if you wish purposely to weaken your impact (to appear less threatening or reduce involvement with the other person), don't turn completely to converse—point your knees away.

- Let your eyes lead. When a martial artist throws his opponent, his eyes look in the direction of the throw. Looking back while moving forward weakens the movement considerably. This works mentally as well. When you're going to execute any strong action or introduce a new program, look ahead. Don't allow yourself to dwell on past movements or mistakes.

- Use counter motions. As you walk, notice which arm swings forward with which leg. In balanced walking, the arms and legs are in opposition: the left arm naturally moves with the right foot and the right arm with the left foot. These counter motions keep you balanced from side to side.

- Avoid static postures. Holding rigid poses is hard on your body. Moreover, others may see you as inflexible (or change-resistant).

- Break up repetition. Machines are designed for repetition, but people thrive on variation. Doing a lot of phone work? Intersperse personal meetings and paper work into your day.

MENTAL LEVERAGE

In *Zen in the Art of Archery*, kyudo master Awa told student Eugen Herrigel, "To shoot well, you must forget your physical strength and shoot only with your strength of mind." Of course, martial artists first train their bodies, but they know a strong mind is the key to accomplishment under pressure.

"Act as if the goal was [sic] infinity," Awa also taught. "A good bowman shoots farther with a bow of medium power than a soulless bowman with the most powerful bow. The result is not due to the bow but to the presence of mind, to the vitality and the state of alertness with which you shoot."

In the martial arts there is an expression, "big circle, little circle, no circle," that describes levels of expertise. The beginner, it is said, makes large inefficient motions, "big circles." He broadly copies an effective image and toils laboriously, but with poor results.

The advanced student moves in "little circles." She has learned to cleave away unnecessary actions; her movements are crisp, focused, and effective.

Oh, but the Master! He moves in "no circles." Barely seeming to shift, he seems effortlessly always to be in the right position, at the right time. Although he is older and less energetic than the novice, the Master easily dominates the contest.

Effectiveness is a product of energy (time and effort expended) and efficiency. As the martial artist ages, he loses the edge of energy and naturally becomes slower. But the expert more than makes up for this by moving in smaller circles. Rather than jumping two feet away from an oncoming punch, he avoids it by two inches. Many martial artists have reported that they began to understand their art only when they could no longer rely on youthful speed and strength.

Small motions are faster, concentrating rather than wasting power. Bruce Lee, a relatively small man, developed a "One Inch Punch" that, without wind-up, could send much larger opponents reeling.

To develop your power and effectiveness, like the martial arts expert, you can use natural laws, physics, and human forces to great benefit in managing.

High- and Low-Leverage Activities

You may have seen a karate expert break bricks, wood, or ice as part of a martial arts demonstration. All of his body weight is focused on a small area. This concentration of force is sufficient to shatter hard materials without harm to the martial artist.

In much the same way, concentration of our energy and force is useful in resolving problems at work. It's easy to become side-tracked in the daily press of meetings, reports, and contacts. We may be deluded into thinking that our job is defined by these activities. But as Intel President Andrew Grove says, "activity is not output."

Managers who believe their role is only to hold meetings, supervise staff, discipline, hire and fire—in short, to fulfil all the traditional managerial responsibilities—are missing the point. The job of any manager is to make sure his unit produces the necessary product or service that moves the organization toward its mission; not his daily activities nor what he *personally* does. This applies to a multinational corporation, a division, or just the two people he supervises.

Grove notes, in *High Output Management*, three ways to get the most output from what you do.

- Influence one person over a long period of time. Examples include teaching a technique to someone *when they really need it*, making motivating performance appraisals, promoting, or delegating wisely.

- Influence many people simultaneously. Hold carefully prepared meetings or training sessions. Communicate via memo, videotape, or electronic mail, and enlist the grapevine to spread information.

- Influence many people over a long period of time. Nipping problems in the bud, doing necessary research and strategic planning, hiring, making timely decisions, assigning a new supervisor—all qualify.

Don't take any of these ordinary activities lightly. Each can augment the returns on your efforts. However using the leverage can also have negative effects. It is possible to

- Create negative conflict. By punishing or dominating others in front of their peers, you can create long-term enemies or a group of detractors.

- De-motivate someone for a long time. Name-calling, perfunctory performance reviews, giving new employees sink-or-swim orientations, meddling or bailing someone out of a needed learning opportunity, failing to recognize extra effort, and insincerely delegating tasks demoralize or reduce motivation.

- Squander many people's time by being unprepared for meetings or arranging useless training.

- Adversely affect many people for a long time. This may be the result of spreading a negative attitude, planning poorly, conducting inadequate market research, avoiding decisions, or any other action that seriously jeopardizes organizational survival.

To become a more effective manager, concentrate on positive high-leverage activities that use measured force, at the critical moment, and in the precise location to move toward the desired direction.

Measured force. People often apply far more force than is required; they use a cannon to kill flies. The master knows not to hard-block the incoming punch two feet away; deflecting it a safe six inches away is enough. Using too much force not only wastes effort, it is also dangerous. A trained opponent can counteract an overly forceful block by spinning around the contact point to deliver a devastating kick or strike. Similarly, too much force in managing may provoke resistance or counter-attack.

William Burroughs' essay, "The Discipline of D.E." (in his book, *The Exterminator*), is based upon the principle of measured force. His main character discovered D.E., Do Easy. "D.E. simply means doing everything you do in the *easiest* and most relaxed manner you can achieve at the time you do it. You can start right now, moving books, sorting papers. Consider the weight of an object. Consider its shape and texture and function and exactly where it belongs. Use the amount of force necessary to get the object from here to there. Don't fumble, jerk, or grab an object."

Burroughs has suggestions for training yourself in the art of D.E.: "Now someone will say . . . 'But if I have to *think* about every move I make' . . . You only have to think and break down movement into a series of still pictures to be studied and corrected because you have not found the easy way. Once you find the easy way, you don't have to think about it. It will almost do itself." Burroughs is right.

D.E. is the way chosen by martial artists and has strong leadership applications. Remember Lao Tsu's recommendations for leading "invisibly." Manage as lightly as you possibly can, not with a heavy hand. You don't have to do everything yourself. In fact, you can't; it's easy to become overwhelmed trying. Instead, encourage your creative people. If their ideas are not helpful now, they may be later. Enthusiastic, bright people can adapt inappropriate ideas into useful ones.

Use of measured force has many benefits. You become a model for those you manage in how to use effort wisely. You guard against wasting energy, keep something in reserve for the unexpected, and reduce the conflict caused by "pushing too hard."

At the critical moment. In the martial arts and in managing, timing is crucial. One strike when the opponent is off balance equals repeated attempts at a well-guarded person. For the manager, this applies when dealing with a special problem; early intervention is usually the most effective.

Unfortunately, some managers of my aquaintance don't seem to understand "the critical moment." A hospital administrator, newly appointed to his position, assigned forty-five department managers to various task forces. These ad hoc groups were asked to make specific recommendations that would help the hospital survive in a highly competitive environment.

Each of the nine task forces worked hard for four months, then presented their reports. After this, there was a vacuum in which the administrator neither acknowledged nor reacted to the recommendations.

Finally, after seven months, the administrator issued a general "thank-you-for-your-work-on-the-committee" memorandum. This was too little, too late. By this time, the managers' morale was low. ("Why bother doing anything? He'll just disregard it anyway! Who's

got time for futile tasks?") Just as important, the administrator's credibility plummeted. The best thanks come when people are receptive and
interested, not when they are disenchanted or their guard is up.

In the precise location. Martial artists aim for precision, knowing
that "close" may not be enough. So they study pressure points to probe
and target areas where they can aim the attack.

Similarly, when A-dec's Phil Westover is looking for ways to institute a new process, he looks for where it will do the most good. After
extensive study, Phil was convinced that motion analysis techniques
could boost productivity in dental chair assembly. (Phil previously
employed this same method at a Western Electric Plant to improve
assemblers' efficiency from one hundred percent of the "company
efficient standard" to three hundred percent!) But motion analysis has
been traditionally resisted by employees—except those paid on a piece-
work basis. Workers often resent having the entire process closely
observed, and measured, and then being told to change their methods.
So Phil knew that grassroots acceptance was needed for the motion
analysis to take hold. But could he sell this to employees?

First, Phil approached the natural leaders among them to see if they
were interested in volunteering to be video-taped doing their jobs.
Most of these staff members were honoured to be asked. Each volunteer
performed the same task three different ways, non-evaluatively labelled
X, Y, and Z.

Then Phil approached a carefully selected sampling of those work
groups most likely to be receptive. Group volunteers viewed the tapes
with Phil. Together they recorded the times required for the task. Each
group assessed the strengths and weaknesses of the X, Y, and Z
approaches.

For the groups so requesting it, Phil taught the motion analysis
principle involved, that is, how they could work more efficiently. Soon,
productivity zoomed.

Phil was effective where others might not have been. He selected the
location where change was needed. By approaching the most influential individuals (using willing volunteers) and selecting receptive work
groups, Phil turned a small experiment into wide-spread company
productivity gains—an excellent demonstration of leverage use.

Toward the desired direction. Judo practitioners must know how
to position the attacker so he will fall, no matter how large he may be.
Besides knowing opponents' *kuzushi* (balance points), judo students

quickly learn that a strong push won't necessarily bring an adversary to the ground. A lateral force pushes a balanced attacker back, not down. It may sound simple, but students spend years in practice learning that they have to aim their force *down* to get the opponent to fall.

Everything you do should move you a step closer to your goals. As in bicycling, using leverage here means making a small push that puts you many strides closer to your destination. "Doing Easy" means eliminating unnecessary tasks and ones that cannot be completed: these only distract you and drain energy. Also, make the most of your creative energy by concentrating on high-leverage activities.

By using martial arts leverage methods, you can magnify your power to accomplish what you'd previously believed was beyond you.

Using Leverage: Techniques for Action

- Observe those who have a strong influence on others. Watch how they carry themselves and move. Compare this to your own movements. Consider getting video-taped as you go through any task; critically review the tape, and watch your posture and movements.

- Concentrate on your hara to increase your calmness and balance during challenging times.

- Select one breathing technique and practise it daily. Note the immediate and longer-term effects.

- Control your posture. Note how adopting different postures affects you and others.

- When doing anything—writing or listening, etc—practise moving as little as you comfortably can while still being effective. Incorporate this into hobbies and other activities. Check to see if you are doing things as "easy" as you can. Practice opening doors and moving objects as effortlessly as possible.

- Focus on output, not activity. Allocate time to high-leverage activities. Periodically monitor yourself to check if you are expending minimal effort to make strides toward your goals. If not, consider switching methods or goals.

PART II

MANAGING PEOPLE

When a person enters upon an undertaking, he prays fervently that he will achieve success in it. Further, he knows that he needs the help of others; success is not to be attained alone.

Gichin Funakoshi, *Karate-do: My Way of Life*

CHAPTER FOUR

The Power of Do: Harnessing Commitment to a Mission

The power of commitment is wondrous and can transcend all other forces.

Tak Kubota, *The Art of Karate*

"The point is at hand. The bandits steal our food, take our daughters and wives, and kill us at their whim. This can continue no longer. There is one way out. Their leader has offered to meet one of us in combat. You have been chosen."

The listener felt both fear and pride. The others before him had fought to their deaths.

"But master, how can I succeed where others failed? Some were as skilled as I, and of greater heart."

"Do not misjudge your courage. It will be there abundantly when the need presents itself. You must be victorious now or we will lose our homes. Our lives and those of our children depend on you. Keep this in mind and fight swiftly and surely."

The man prepared himself, with steadfast practice. He dedicated his life to his family and his friends, and went into combat.

The contest was long. The man was overmatched in experience by the bandit chief. *Shuto* chops fell and were parried. The bandit's superior strength seemed to wear down the village champion. But when fear threatened to disable him, the young man remembered his master's words and drew power from his mission. He defeated the bandit and saved his village.

Martial artists derive strength from their *do* (pronounced doh), which means their Way of Life. Judo is The Way of Yielding; Kendo, the Way of the Sword; Tae Kwon Do, The Foot-Fist Way; and Aikido, The Way of Harmonious Forces.

"Traditionally the Way is what absorbs man's whole being," writes Michael Random in *The Martial Arts*. "The Way, moreover, gives the idea of a constant but unending attempt at one's own perfection."

For many, the martial arts are a spiritual path that emphasizes connection to nature and to God. The credo of the International Karate Association states, "The power of karate comes from the God within." Aikido founder Morihei Ueshiba said, "True *budo* (martial arts) is at one with the universe, which means being united with the centre of the universe. True budo is a labour of love. It involves giving life to all that exists and not killing or opposing one another. We progress in life with this strength of spirit and we strive to maintain a global view of the world."

Power dedication to the do can be felt by others. Master Tak Kubota wrote, "There is a level of purpose in karate that manifests itself as an 'aura' which cannot be seen or touched—it is sensed. . . . No one would dare attack." This is not mystical double-talk. Many martial arts anecdotes attest to masters who were "unattackable" because of their highly developed *wa* (internal harmony). I have seen Mitsugi Saotome demonstrate this. He calls forth a black-belt student to rush and attack him. But Saotome does not move out of the way. He calmly smiles and placidly offers his hand. The attacker actually forgets his original intent and shakes the Master's hand. He feels extremely foolish when he realizes he has been so easily diverted from his charge. There is no point in attacking someone totally confident and calm; you know you can't win.

The Way of the samurai is the way of power. It is also the way of protection and love. Discipline is continuous. Commitment to mission helps the warrior hold to his or her path, not letting the attention stray too far. What do martial artists do when they feel disconnected and at odds with the world? Train, spar, practise kata (fighting form), and meditate.

In practising martial methods, the students' bodies get used and somewhat abused. They endure twisted wrists, pulled hair, punches, and kicks. As one martial arts student quipped, "In the martial arts you let your friends beat you up so that other people can't." Understandably, there are times when martial artists ask why they put in so much time and endure such discomfort.

A sense of mission helps overcome pain or adversity. It puts discomfort into perspective as the price of reaching a higher goal. Just when it appears their resources are depleted, martial artists call on their secret weapon—their strength of purpose. Commitment to a higher purpose unleashes a power that bolsters strength and provides the necessary perspective.

Martial artists are mission- and value-driven, whether their mission is to protect others, heighten their harmony with nature, increase self-understanding, or master fear. It is their source of inspiration and motivation. This sense of mission and purpose is equally useful on the battlefield, in the boardroom, or in the plant.

As a manager, your mission, should you decide to accept it, is to harness commitment, your own and those of others, to create a vital organization. Enlist ideals in your work life. As you begin to control yourself, develop your own do, your own *Way of Management.*

THE WAY OF BUSINESS

A martial arts feat, such as breaking a brick, requires a mission. When you break a board or brick, you demonstrate, mostly to yourself, that your inner power, and your confidence in that power, can get through things, even hard objects that you feared might injure you. All doubt must be transcended, all power dedicated to the action. If you let your focus drift, even for an instant, force will not be correctly transmitted and your hand can be badly hurt.

Have you ever gone the extra distance, worked on a special project, or given time to a worthy cause? Have you really extended yourself and felt great about it? Why didn't you complain or feel overstressed? You tapped a special kind of power because you felt committed, and that what you were doing was important.

Some feel just the opposite—that they are going through the motions, marking time, not accomplishing anything worthwhile. They wake up thinking about the meaninglessness of their jobs, as if the week were too long or Monday had many more hours in it than Friday.

At seminars, I often poll executives about their concerns. They often select as a major issue "not sure if my work has real meaning." Privately, many managers report feeling alienated, powerless, and without direction. Loss of motivation is not only the benchmark of the mediocre; successful, intelligent executives also suffer from it. For these managers, work has become either a necessary grind or an individual crusade. How much can I attain? How far can I go? What recognition may I accrue? This "how-much" motivation can be difficult to sustain.

If you want to avoid this depressing rut, or if you, like martial arts experts, want to convert the merely adequate into something special, you can develop focus by articulating a mission and set of values.

For example, many managers and employees of the U.S. Postal Service report that the organization has often been marked by low morale. But come the Christmas season, employee morale improves impressively, even though the workload multiplies. Why? Because, as one employee explains, "This is the time we live for. We have a real mission—to carry the holiday spirit."

Never underestimate the power of dedication to a mission. In a negative sense, the fanatical commitment of the terrorist enables a small number of individuals to hold sway over many. Although they are deluded extremists, there is something to learn from their determination. You can, with wisdom, tap the power of commitment in a healthy and meaningful manner for yourself and those you manage. You can find it, hone it, and direct it.

Lao Tsu's *Tao Te Ching* ("Book of the Way") is an ancient treatise on effective leadership. (Tao is Chinese for do.) Business can be a do, a Way of Life, dedicated to developing resources, providing services, and improving the quality of living. Like the martial-arts counterpart, a black-belt manager is mission-driven. They both know that mission gives power and makes life worth living.

Karate master Tak Kubota writes, in *The Art of Karate*, "To each his viewpoint of his experience, to all the common path of their goal." A common mission and set of values can help align people toward the organizational goal. A common purpose makes an organization more than a mass of people going in different directions, performing overlapping or disconnected tasks.

Government manager Bill Thomas concurs. Like most martial artists, Bill enlists mission and values. He is an intelligent, skilled communicator, and a voracious reader. Bill is determined to make his state agency an excellent service organization, on a par with the business world's elite.

"It's absolutely essential in any organization," he says, "for the top management to create a mission, for all employees to know where they're going. It's probably more pervasive and influential than anything else top management can do. Each of our 'missioned' employees can turn the wheel to steer the organization where it's going. So you don't have to turn it by yourself or wrestle it away from them. They do the work, too.

"A mission is like looking through a telescope; it tells you where you're going. It can also be a mirror. By looking at a mission, you can tell whether your actions are consistently in line with the organization's good."

Like the martial artist, you can start by formulating a personal mission. Such a belief system provides perspective on the countless minor struggles of business life. An important contract has suddenly been cancelled? Tax code changes are cutting into profitability? Competition is mounting? Take solace in your mission. Remind yourself of your purpose. Don't allow pressure-produced, tunnel vision to stall your productivity or destroy your motivation. One manager has developed a professional mission of "helping people work together." Another manager's mission is "helping my staff grow." My own mission is "to serve as a force for positive change—improving effectiveness and morale."

Black-belt managers keep their mission statement on their desk or wall and turn to it during trying times. They repeat the mission to themselves each morning and twice on days when they wonder why they are bothering to show up at work at all.

Balance is vital for effectiveness in both the martial arts and in managing. An idealistic visionary may be able to look ahead into the future, and keep the long-range perspective. However, his weakness is in dealing with details and completing the daily job.

Then there are those without a higher purpose. People who study martial arts only to dominate others don't usually progress far. Similarly, some people in the work place are bereft of vision and can see no purpose beyond reacting to circumstances from one day to the next. Their narrow perspective prevents them from reaching beyond daily problems, and it limits what they can accomplish.

Don't allow yourself to become fixed at either of these extremes. Remember your do and practise the details of your art every day. Stay balanced and look ahead. Develop a mission and a set of values that you can apply in real life, that help you get the daily job done and then help you to continue to become something more.

AN EFFECTIVE MISSION STATEMENT

By design, mission statements are idealistic and general. They point to a destination for the organization, and a mission also indicates an organization's values. Morihei Ueshiba stated his art's mission simply: "Aikido is the realization of love."

On a black-belt exam, a martial artist is evaluated by two criteria—his spirit and his technique. Techniques, like objectives, are easier to assess. Is he balanced? Does he exhibit control? Are his movements small and effective?

The spirit, which many masters consider more important, is more difficult to see. One does not gauge it in the same way as *waza* (technique). Does the artist exude purpose, dedication? Is he calm under attack, showing a winning spirit? Or is he overproud of his power and prone to use excessive force?

Similarly, mission statements are a matter of the spirit and should *not* include goals or objectives which are measurable and specific. Goals generally have one- to five-year outcomes and focus on behavioural output. Objectives are specific actions that bring you closer to your goals.

For example, profitability can be either a goal or an objective (a vehicle of ensuring that the mission continues to be fulfilled). So "getting a fifteen percent return on investment" and "increasing market share" may be important goals. If your organization does not make an adequate profit, it may not be able to remain in business to fulfil its mission of "improving the quality of life in our community." Few people are driven to accomplish purely monetary goals; the mission must enlist a broader spectrum of support from all staff.

In the story at the beginning of this chapter, we might define the man's mission as "protecting the lives of his family and neighbours." The best mission statements are well defined, inspirational, easily understood on an emotional level, communicated well to employees and public, and consistently applied. If the statement is meant to arouse staff spirit it has to become part of their thinking. It won't if it's not understandable, or uses language that distances people from the desired action.

There is currently much literature on mission statements that is overly theoretical and insufficiently useful. For example, many organizations already have mission statements that are too long and complex. I usually ask managers in seminars if their organization has a mission statement. Then I ask those who do have a mission to repeat it. This is a test. A good mission statement has to be easily memorized and stated. If the statement is too long or vague to be easily recalled, there is, in effect, no operating mission statement.

Mission statements such as "to provide needed services to clients, disseminate information, propagate a climate of trust and cooperation among employees, and be a responsible community member" are too long to remember. Some companies' statements are even longer and more diffuse than this.

Be practical: think like a martial artist. Move your mission in "small circles" to get the most done. In the martial arts, short focused punches are generally more effective ones. Similarly, the punch of a mission statement lies in its brevity. Keep it brief and simple. All kinds of employees will be able to understand and embrace it. On the other hand, simplicity does not ensure clarity. One large company has the mission statement "Serving our clients better." This statement can easily be interpreted in contradictory ways. Better than what? What is good enough? Are the clients current or prospective? If it's too vague, the mission will have little meaning.

Aim for internal consistency. If your mission as a hospital is "to improve health and well-being in our community and in the world," it is crucial that you also improve the health of your employees and their families. Otherwise credibility and morale will plummet.

Like many mission-oriented organizations, Bill Thomas' agency publishes a booklet for staff and the public. "Our Values" is the heading on the mission statement's first page. Typically, such value-driven organizations emphasize the human element. To further explain the mission, other major headings in the booklet include "The Commission's Most Important Asset is People," "Working Together," and "To Serve the Public."

The most effective mission statements focus on serving or helping. For example, the mission of an accounting firm might be "raising our client's standard of living"; that of a trucking line, "transporting needed materials."

VALUES AND PROFIT: THE A-DEC *DO*

Judo master Henry Seishiro Okazaki wrote, in an unpublished paper, "every student of Judo should realize that honesty is the foundation of all virtues. Kindness is the secret of business prosperity. Amiability is the essence of success. Working pleasantly is the mother of health. Strenuous effort and diligence conquer adverse circumstances. Simplicity and fortitude are the keys to joy and gladness; and service to humanity is the fountain of mutual existence and common prosperity."

Values are not just for the martial arts or government agencies. Managing by values can be profitable as well. Ken and Joanne Austin own one such "value-driven" company, A-dec, the largest manufacturer of dental equipment in the United States. Joanne and Ken started out modestly; they now own A-dec's industrial park, all one hundred acres of it.

Their mission is articulated in "The A-dec Way," a powerful values statement. Because of its richness, clarity, and proven effectiveness as a management tool, their statement is summarized here.

Striving for Excellence: At A-dec our working philosophy is a commitment to strive for excellence in all we do. Recognizing the need to maintain control of our future, we looked inside A-dec to define the secret of our past success and as a result developed the "A-dec Way." The A-dec Way is a written expression of the operating philosophy which governs all aspects of our company.

Fifteen "principles of concern" and six "questions of test" make up the A-dec Way:

1. Demonstrate concern for people
2. Provide for opportunity and assist in self-development
3. Provide an atmosphere encouraging self-satisfaction and pride
4. Encourage team effort
5. Maintain complete fairness, honesty, and integrity
6. Maintain open, consistent, and regular communication
7. Encourage public service
8. Encourage creativity
9. Commit ourselves to productivity and quality

10. Maintain consistency
11. Dedication to improvement
12. Keep things simple and basic
13. Build on a basis of "need"
14. Give attention to detail
15. Conserve resources

Questions:

1. Is there a need?
2. Is this the simplest and best way to do it?
3. Am I using time and material effectively?
4. Am I helping make A-dec better for everyone?
5. Can I be proud of what we are doing?
6. Have I communicated?

This statement reads a lot like Musashi's nine guidelines. And having worked with A-dec over six years, I've seen that while the organization is not problem free, it really does follow the A-dec Way. The company is down-to-earth and doing very well. I have spoken to many A-dec employees, past and present. They all describe A-dec as a special place. Most former workers have regretted leaving.

Values in A-dec are shown in the little things. Employees are paid well, and they are expected to perform accordingly. A premium is placed on flexibly adjusting to an employee's individual needs. A-dec provides free coffee to its staff, its plant is exceptionally clean, and cafeteria and grounds are beautifully maintained. Job-relevant education and training are provided; promotion from within is encouraged. Courses are also offered on personal development, usually on an employee's own time.

In the early 1980s, A-dec experimented with Group Technology. Traditional assembly-line job roles in which one employee drilled holes and another bolted together dental chair components were replaced by a team effort. In the new arrangement, a group of employees was responsible for producing a prescribed number of chairs. All employees in that unit were trained in all assembly functions. Consistent with the A-dec philosophy, the first Group Technology "family" was composed of volunteers.

The experiment was a rousing success. Not only did productivity skyrocket, other employees pressed to have their functions reformatted into groups. And the timetable for conversion to this process was shortened by years.

As you might expect in an entrepreneurial company, creativity is predominant. A-dec has moved from its first product, vacuum drills, to a full line of dental chairs and equipment, and even to vacuum locks for use in prisons and industry.

Tours for visiting executives interested in A-dec's black-belt management style are regularly provided by the company's Personnel/Training manager, Phil Westover. Why, I once asked Phil, does he take valuable time to do this? What's in it for A-dec? He said there are two benefits. First, Ken and Joanne Austin have made a commitment to spreading effective management to businesses and people everywhere. Second, employees take pride in being a model to others. They know that their hard work maintains this status.

Visiting managers come away believing that many A-dec methods can be successfully adapted to large corporations as well as to the public sector. As in A-dec's case, a combination of idealistic values and high-quality management can lead to great success.

DEVELOPING THE MISSION AND VALUES

While the martial arts embody a general path, a mission that has been developed over centuries, for a mission to spread power, it has to be individualized, personally refined, and wholeheartedly accepted by the martial artist himself.

This means that inconsistencies must be resolved. Walter Muryasz writes, in *Precepts of the Martial Artist*, "the martial arts may be the path [that one] has chosen to self-understanding, but he must never lose sight of the fact that his art, its use and original purpose, was born in the reality of violence. For the martial artist, to lose sight of this fact is to lose the foundation which gives the art its life, vitality, and its purpose for being. The reality may have been born in violence, but the purpose is harmony and the end of conflict. Somewhere between the two points, the artist is himself changed—reborn—the flower of the art."

Equally for the manager, the act of formulating a mission statement is both difficult and enlightening. "Developing a mission is the most important thing an organization can do and one of the best tools in making a cultural shift," says Larry Jacobson, training director for a public agency. "But it is not an easy task. It took our top managers a full week off-site to develop the mission and goals. And there was considerable acrimony during the process. Although this was uncomfortable, it was very valuable. It showed us we really had no clear understanding or acceptance of our direction at that time."

Frequently, when an organization takes the time to articulate its values, it becomes clear that staff members have conflicting ideas of what the organization is about, where it should be going, and what it should be doing. This is uncomfortable. But, just as the martial artist must train to go beyond discomfort, confronting conflicts in values is crucial to resolving the problem of working at cross-purposes.

Longer mission statements are often compromises that result because management is unwilling to struggle with the difficult process of reaching a consensus. Instead of weaving various points of view into a short statement of consensus, everyone's ideas are combined into a massive document. The result is an unfocused mission that nobody actually uses. Time is wasted, and it arouses staff suspicions about organizational disunity.

There are several ways of fusing the mission. It may be written by a small group of top managers, or by a committee of managers and line staff. The board of directors should also be involved in formulating and approving the mission. Lead the board through exercises that help them visualize where the organization is, where it's going, how it will get there. Also ask for employees' help developing your mission statement; their involvement will transfer into commitment.

Remember, as does the martial artist, that true motivation and change come from within. If the mission is to be a vehicle for internal motivation and change, it is best to solicit comments from all staff on the first draft. Don't be too attached to the initial draft.

How you solicit input is important. Make yourself available to employees for response to the mission. Present your request for feedback as if you were driving a train. You are moving a focused, powerful organization to its destination. You can take one of several parallel tracks, but no one person can derail the train. Make it clear in advance who was involved in drafting the mission and what points of view you considered. Say you are looking for adjustments, not a whole-scale reformatting. Staff may make suggestions, but at this point they will most likely be minor changes of wording.

WHAT TO DO WHEN THE MISSION
DOESN'T TAKE HOLD

Only beginners—martial artists or managers—believe their initial technique will always hold sway. Experts know how to recover from adversity, to counter resistance to their moves.

Once you publicize the mission, some staff are likely to respond negatively or remain uncommitted. Their reactions may have several possible meanings. Each can be dealt with.

1. They don't comprehend how the mission statement translates into action. Do they have an opportunity to see how the organization fulfils its mission? Adjust their position just as a martial artist does to position an opponent. Place these employees in an area where they can see the good your organization does.

2. They don't feel the tasks they perform have any relationship to the mission statement. Remind them of their purpose. Help them see the connection, how their job plays a needed part in fulfilling the mission.

3. They don't see the mission statement as honestly reflecting the organization's purpose. Like a judo expert, make resistance work for you. Staff who spot inconsistencies can help to strengthen your organization. Incorporate their ideas, if valid, into the mission and goals.

4. They don't like the direction in which the organization is moving. Like a sumo wrestler, control your space; stand firm. Help them find a better place to work, if necessary. This is the time to be honest about your organization's direction. As Larry Jacobson says, "We had to bluntly tell these people, 'If you're mildly uncomfortable with this mission, you will probably be even more uncomfortable in this organization in two years, and find it intolerable in five.' "

5. They basically mistrust top management. This is often due to lingering unresolved problems. If you sense this to be the case and you value the employee, cut to the heart of the matter. Spend some time clearing the air so you can deal with the underlying issues. Only then will you be able to move freely toward fulfilling the organizational mission.

6. They see top management as inconsistent or hypocritical. Like the wise General, show them your strength. Practise good internal public relations. Be sure to advertise fully all the good things the organization is doing for the public and for employees.

7. They are dissatisfied with their own jobs or career development. Help them move. Is it time for them to find a more satisfying position? Are there internal vehicles for job enrichment or redesign? Is there adequate promotion from within? Are criteria for advancement clear and fair?

The dissenters may be a small and vocal minority. See who your real opponents and allies are. Don't make the mistake of focusing too much attention on a small percentage of dissatisfied employees. There are some in any organization. Use good sampling techniques to check the *overall* response to the mission.

When you have a final draft, publish the mission widely. Put it on letterhead, place it atop the agenda for all meetings, hang it on bulletin boards and in offices, and reinforce it in employee newsletters. Once the mission and values are published, there will always be some people looking for inconsistencies. These complaints are valuable. Don't fight or deny them. Parry them and use them.

Government agency head Bill Thomas handles it this way: "When employees tell me I've been inconsistent with our mission, I admit it, if they're right. These confrontations help me see where I've been out of line. I tell them our mission is not a photograph of where we are now. If you're saying we're not living up to the mission statement, you're correct. It's a vision of where we'd like to be, what we're moving toward. As George Bernard Shaw said, 'When I point the way ahead of you, I am also pointing ahead of me.'

"The worst thing you can do is stick to your guns because you don't want to lose credibility. [This will make things worse if they've really caught you.] But you can turn this to your favour. You can show you've got a record of being honest, open-minded, and flexible.

"It's not going to work all the time. I'm sure some see me as weak or wishy-washy. But if you're going to gear your life according to the lowest common denominator, you're doomed! You do the best you can."

Equally important, these seeming detractors are often idealistic "mission watchdogs." Although they start off being disgruntled about a seeming inconsistency or unfairness, they frequently wind up becoming strong proponents of the mission.

What about those who leave out of dissatisfaction with the mission statement? Don't bad-mouth them; here's another opportunity to show consistency with the mission. Besides, former employees sometimes work for or become customers. Defuse their disgruntlement by treating them fairly. No organization needs angry ex-employees looking for ways to get back at the company.

Most important, remaining staff are watching how you treat those who leave. "Is the mission sincere or just a manipulation?" "If they treated her that way, how will they treat me?" "Do I want to work for this organization?"

USING THE MISSION STATEMENT

Martial expertise combines philosophy with the development of true reactions—moving without thought to avoid an unexpected kick. This kind of skill takes time to develop and refine. Similarly, implementing a good mission statement is not easy. How often does a managerial team spend hundreds of hours developing a mission statement only to file or post it and then forget it exists?

To inspire and align staff, the mission statement has to become part of daily work activity. Studies show the spirit and attitude of top managers is the most influential factor in organizational morale. So implementing the mission must start by making sure that upper-level managers have the kinks worked out and that they wholeheartedly support the mission. If top managers don't really believe in the mission, then mid-level managers and line staff won't either.

Educate and train all managers in the import and power of the mission as a living tool, not just an exercise. Remind them how martial artists turn their mission into power.

A mission becomes an internal guide system that reminds you of priorities during times of uncertainty or difficulty. Making decisions during stressful times can be dangerous; such plans may be good only in unusual circumstances. These schemes are the result of what many call "managing by crisis," "knee-jerk management," or "being in a reactive mode."

Consider the mission statement before making crucial and long-term plans. This way, your decisions are more likely to be in line with your desired direction. You'll retain your perspective, reduce decision-making stress, and stay on target.

Using the mission as much as possible is the best way to sell it to your employees and to the world:

Remind yourself of the mission. Set goals and objectives that directly help your organization achieve its mission.

Use the mission to allocate time among competing activities. Ask yourself, "Does this activity help us get closer to fulfilling our mission?" If not, give it a lower priority and less of your time than more mission-oriented activities.

Resolve conflict by referring to the mission. Look for a common ground based on a mission that is greater than any dispute.

Remind employees that their service helps accomplish the mission. Receptionists are not merely greeting people, and computer staff are not just processing data. *Every staff member* plays a vital role in helping the organization fulfil its mission.

It is important that staff see the positive effects of fulfilling the mission. All staff, especially those in service industries, need to see, hear, and feel the results of their efforts—the woman whose life was saved because of the fire extinguisher you manufacture or the once-feuding family now reunited with your communication company's help. Because many internal staff are too removed from the customer to see the results, the organization must be their eyes and ears, bringing them these morale-boosting anecdotes.

Be sure to publicize any customer letters pertaining to the mission, such as those thanking employees or reflecting on how your company's goods and services have helped them. Also ask staff with direct customer contact (sales, customer service, repair) to pass along stories of satisfied customers or examples of your mission at work in the world. After internally publicizing one of these mission success stories, thank *all* staff for their efforts. The purpose is to help all employees commit themselves to the mission, not just those on the firing line. When telling of the boy who was healed at your hospital, don't thank just the medical staff. Also acknowledge the clerical staff who did the necessary scheduling, those who facilitated the required insurance clearance, and the employees who supported family members during the procedure. Everyone in the organization helped get the job done.

Encourage employees to develop their own mission statements to help them have greater success and sustain them during hard times. When such times come and morale is down, remind employees of their part in the mission. Mid-level managers can also develop mission statements for their departments. Of course, they should be consistent with the organization's mission.

Use the mission statement to encourage staff to grow. When managers ask about solving a problem, refer them to the mission. By encouraging them to apply it, you will help make them better managers.

Publicize it. In an interview with *The New York Times*, IBM's CEO John Akers stated, "IBM will be permitted to grow and prosper only where people and governments understand that we are indeed *helping to solve society's problems.*"

A mission can attract prospective employees and value-driven investors. Include it in advertising. Ralston-Purina's "helping pets live longer, healthier lives" has been effectively used in advertising.

Incorporate the mission into your company logo and corporate graphics. For example, a food processing company might display pictures of an accomplished mission such as families at holiday dinners, children eating, or people enjoying shopping. Some organizations have even commissioned company songs that are written along these lines.

Developing and applying a mission helps you climb the mountain. An idealistic and accurate mission statement will concentrate your power to break through the organizational bricks of inertia, dissension, and uncertainty.

Techniques for Action: Harnessing the Power of Do:

- Develop a personal mission that you are dedicated to. Share this with a trusted friend. Start thinking in terms of your own mission. Make sure that you are living what you deeply believe in. Apply your personal mission as a guide in professional and personal activities.

- As a martial artist does before a critical fight, note where you are afraid or disillusioned. Then remind yourself of your mission.

- Remember the martial relation between having a strong purpose and being "unattackable." When you feel besieged, ask yourself, "Is this happening because my 'level of purpose' is weak?"

- Tour an organization whose mission and values are well-defined. Ask hard questions. ("How did you get to this point? What problems do you have with the mission and values? What should we watch for in our own company?")

- Be a martial General to your staff. Help them develop a mission and set of values for your organization, department, or group. Discipline yourself to refrain from imposing values on them. Instead, help draw them out. When you have the mission and values, spread them around. Use them at every opportunity.

• Check your business code of ethics for consistency with the mission.

• Bring organizational inconsistencies to the surface. Make them fair game for staff discussion. Seek an honest resolution of the inconsistencies.

• Remind yourself of times you have broken through fearsome barriers. Assess what provided you with the power. Remember this strength is inside you, awaiting your call.

CHAPTER FIVE

Motivating Through Softness and Hardness

Karate is like a flower . . . sometimes soft, sometimes fierce.

From the credo of the International Karate Association

When you watch martial arts experts throw larger opponents to the ground, you do not see an exhibition of blind force. They *don't* fight the opponent's momentum or block his strength. Against a stronger or faster opponent, they could be quickly overpowered. Rather, they control themselves, staying calm and ready for the right opportunity *to move* their opponent to the ground. Expert martial artists create their opportunities for moving another by how they themselves move. The same is true for master managers, and the same martial arts principles, applied in a controlled manner, can be used to inspire an employee or colleague.

Most managers I've encountered sincerely want to motivate their employees to do their jobs creatively and enthusiastically. They strive for higher productivity, stronger customer relations, and improved morale. Yet we often see articles such as these from *The Wall Street Journal*: "Loyalty Ebbs At Many Companies As Employees Grow Disillusioned," or "More Honesty Tests Used To Gauge Workers' Morale." Why, many managers ask, are people not motivated? What do I have to do to reach them?

Here are several martial arts strategies for creating movement you can apply to staff motivation:

- Knowing what doesn't work: don't create resistance
- Balance softness and hardness
- Create and steer movement by the soft power of invitation

- Adjust the work climate for better movement
- Strengthen your team

KNOWING WHAT DOESN'T WORK: HOW NOT TO CREATE RESISTANCE

For centuries, the martial disciplines have critically observed how people react. Walter Muryasz, a master of physical movement, writes in *Precepts of the Martial Artist*, "The way of movement not only deals with the movement of the body, but also the movement of the mind. To know the movement of the opponent's mind, study the movement of your own mind. Know how the conscious mind reacts and deals with the thoughts and feelings that the unconscious mind throws up to it, and how it dictates your physical responses."

Begin by observing yourself. Notice how you resist excessive force directed at you. Watch others. It doesn't matter who they are, crafts people or clerical staff, or where they work, in offices or in the field. People resist when they are pushed too hard.

Martial artists deal with forces. In a practical sense, they understand Newton's Third Law of Dynamics: For every action, there is an equal and opposite reaction. Simply put, force creates resistance; this is an unconscious reaction.

As an experiment, face a partner and place your hands together palm-to-palm. Without warning, let one of you push hard. Notice the reaction. When one pushes, the other pushes back. Sometimes he responds with more force.

While we may not physically push on others or get pushed in return, a lot of this does go on at work, mentally and emotionally. Even when the pushing is not physical, the response is the same. Motivating by pushing increases resistance and escalates conflict.

Many organizations are mired in productivity-draining resistance caused by overly aggressive managers and supervisors. Kurt Lewin, a behavioural scientist who applies physical principles (he called it "Field Theory") to industrial management, labelled managers who exert coercive influence "superchargers." These supervisors, Lewin found, are indeed able to make their employees work. *But only when the employees feel the direct presence of the boss.* Naturally, the boss can only be in one place at a time. Employees stop working whenever the boss is somewhere else, whether it's just around the corner, or on vacation, or merely not checking their work. Also, coercing one or two employees is one thing, but pushing a group to perform is an overwhelming task.

How can this approach work with more than a handful of people to supervise? To be effective, this style of motivation may require a large number of watchdog supervisors. The trend, however, in many organizations is toward reducing the number of supervisors; therefore supercharging won't be feasible.

Under the too watchful eye of a boss, coerced employees do only the bare minimum. They don't take risks or try to be creative. This is a classic manœuvre of resistance, so effective that it is often used, especially in Europe, as an alternative to strike action. It is called "work to rule," which means following the rules to the letter. Similarly, you may hear an employee say, "I'm sorry, that's not in my job description," which is just another form of resistance.

Like most traditional motivation strategies, the supercharger approach puts employees under more stress. Breathe down their necks, drill it into them until they get it, and make them give you a full day's work for their pay. Is it any wonder employees resist being motivated this way? In a modified supercharger approach, some managers use heavy-handed threats and modest rewards to make people work. If you use the carrot and stick, employees will match your expectations. They'll be as creative and enthusiastic as donkeys.

Technology has updated supercharger methods. Computers can now measure each keystroke an operator enters; electronic eavesdropping on employees' conversations can check their performance. It's no secret when this is done. Predictably, employees rebel. They solicit unionization for protection, file more grievances or workers' compensation claims, or come down with stress-related illnesses. Morale plummets, and drags down the quality of service too.

There's nothing wrong with monitoring work—in fact, it's important to do. But if you use this as a threat, or if you give employees reason to believe you don't trust them, they'll act accordingly. Admittedly, it's easier to overpower some employees more than others—the meek and those with strong needs for approval. But don't also expect these same people to be creative. It just isn't *their* style. The more creative you want your staff to be, the less supercharging makes sense.

If you want employees to develop better, more cost-effective ways to do the job, to adapt to unpredictable situations, or to respond successfully to clients with different needs, reduce coercion.

It doesn't work as a primary strategy. But there are advanced methods that do.

BALANCING SOFTNESS AND HARDNESS FOR MOTIVATIONAL POWER

The Power of Softness

Martial arts masters agree that softness is not weakness, but derives from control. In *Aikido and the Harmony of Nature*, Mitsugi Saotome wrote that students can only attain expertise through balancing hardness with softness:

> In making a fine sword, the iron is continually stressed. Forged in flames, it is softened by the heat of aggression so that shaping and refinement may take place. It is beaten, pounded, folded back upon itself, heated, pounded until all the impurities are driven away. Plunged into water, the temper is set, the fires controlled, and wisdom prepares to sharpen its edge. The process is very complicated and no part can be omitted. Its hidden layers number more than a million. But the finished product is simple and pure of line. It is strong, yet flexible, and its surface reflects all which is around it.
>
> The study [of martial arts], too, is built up layer upon layer. Hard and soft training must both be experienced. If you are always training hard, consumed by fire, you will lose your sensitivity to your partner's reaction, you will begin to ignore the all important thread of communication between you. If you are always training softly, immersed in water, you will never be stressed enough to discover your strength. You will lose reality, you will lose the fire, and you will lose the Way.

Master martial artists generally don't make a big thing about their strengths, their "hard" core that gives them their power. They move like everyone else, without stomping, glaring, puffing up, or otherwise signalling "look how strong I am."

Managers who only know how to rant and rave and pressure their staff to perform are weakened by their limited style. Superficial hardness induces resistance in others and stress in everyone, including the manager. This kind of brittle approach is especially unsuitable to managing the creative staff that is the cornerstone of many organizations.

Martial artists know that a sword left unsheathed loses its edge. Similarly, a perpetually confrontational management style is blunted by automatic resistance or indifference. People get accustomed to the rages of the always blustering manager and learn to ignore them. By comparison, a "soft" style makes chosen movements of confrontation even stronger. Mary Devlin, data processing manager for a large public utility, says, "Of course there are times I stand up on my hind legs and say, 'This is it!' But I try to do that only when it counts. When I do say, 'No!' people pay attention, because I don't say it that often."

Softness is flexible and unthreatening. Think of steel sheathed in velvet. It's gentle and inviting outside, firm yet unbrittle within. You can change your non-verbal demeanour by visualizing yourself as being "covered steel." If you're uncomfortable thinking of yourself as "soft," call it something else. Perhaps you're more comfortable with "flexible." "Subtle management" is what Omark Industries' training manager Janet Lewis says allows work groups to act as independently as possible.

One wise manager looks for "soft power" when promoting. "We go through an extraordinary process when we promote someone from non-manager to the managerial ranks. We look for the courage to be soft, for people who aren't into heavy power. We want managers who have the confidence to make decisions but with the courage to consult with others, to respect higher levels of expertise than they have, and to really consider their staff members without being threatened. It becomes really apparent when you contrast this with the staff sergeant, 'do-it-my-way, do-it-now, end-of-conversation' style we used to have."

A soft style helps you read others' resistance; in contrast, hardness is less sensitive. The person who can sense others' tension and resistance is in a position to use these, judo-like, towards positive ends.

Softness has its healing aspect, too. Some vital points that are used to maim or kill can also heal when palpated in a soft, controlled manner. For example, a tae kwon do method for stopping nose bleeds involves firm gentle pressure at the base of the skull, a place where potentially deadly blows may be delivered. It's a question of control. These vital "healing" spots are points of power. Too much force harms; too little does nothing. Gentle, controlled force animates. The same is true in managing. To bring people alive, learn to apply the right amount of force in the vital areas.

THE SOFT POWER OF INVITATION

Martial artists and master executives don't create unnecessary resistance. They deal with people as "softly" as possible by *inviting* or *influencing*, not controlling, others. Influencing can be done in many ways. In *Precepts of the Martial Artist*, Walter Muryasz writes about moving an attacker where you want him by leading his attention. "The true lead draws the opponent into the space where you want him. To give him what he wants also draws him into that space, but only if you are aware of what he wants. It is the mind you are leading, its intent, conditioning, and perceptions."

Interestingly, "leading" here means "drawing," not pushing or pulling. Muryasz is inviting others to move in a certain direction by understanding and using their natural inclinations.

In organizations, the best leading also works through invitation. Controlling less allows people room for doing more. "Many organizations' staff are overmanaged. Hire people who are bright. Let them know what you expect, then give them freedom to move. Even young people can blossom and don't need as much direction as a lot of administrators think they need," advises Ross Merrick, Executive Director of the National Association for Sport and Physical Education.

Avoid needless control. Be practical. Make only those rules that are absolutely needed. Are dress codes for back room staff necessary? What about rules restraining personal pictures on desks? Are you managing for productivity and profit or for power? Lao Tsu gave a relevant leadership suggestion in the *Tao Te Ching*: "If you allow the person to act, then he develops his abilities."

The manager is in the centre of his business unit; all eyes are on him. When he moves, he invites others to follow. He draws them after him; he takes the lead by doing. He doesn't tell them what to do; he invites them by doing it the desired way himself. His intention and commitment are "hard"; his style is "soft."

Instead of searching for devious ways to get people to move, he asks them. This sometimes converts the most virulent adversary into an ally. For example, he calmly and sincerely approaches a dissident board member prior to an important meeting. ("I really need your help on this for us to prosper.")

There's another reason to manage staff softly as well as firmly. For any organization, high employee morale is vital for smooth, efficient functioning. This is especially true in service organizations where the product is no more than the efforts of its employees. Staff who are dissatisfied cannot deliver as high-quality service to clients and customers as those who have high morale. "If you don't have happy people, you don't get the work done," contends Robert Dernedde, expert manager of a service organization.

Invitational power can also be used to hold together a rapidly growing company whose staff threatens to splinter into special interest groups. Invite them to re-commit themselves to organizational mission, values, and goals.

Using Secondary Pressure

Realistically, like any subtle strategy, invitational power is difficult to master. But its subtlety is its strength. John Clodig teaches black-belt students a concept called "secondary pressure." It means not putting your strength at the point of attack. Mr. Clodig shows that using direct force is inefficient against a strong, prepared attacker. If he grabs your wrist, don't attempt to overpower him with arm strength. This only works when you can clearly overcome your opponent. Even then, sophisticated attackers can counter any reaction they can feel. Instead, put your strength away from the point of attack, where they can't feel it. Move first from your shoulders or hips, not from the point where you are held. This is similar to the "not being trapped" exercise described in the first chapter.

How can you apply secondary pressure in managing? Have you ever wished you could help your boss change, but he rejects anything critical you have to say? You know he will resist *direct* suggestions. So put your pressure where he can't feel it. Find non-threatening ways of approaching him. Leave an article on your desk—or anywhere he is likely to see it—that offers some solutions to his problem; discuss offering staff a training session you know would also benefit him; or, if appropriate, talk to a trusted peer of your boss, or to his friend or spouse.

Clearly, these can be dangerous strategies. Be sure of your own motivations. If you're really trying to harm him or just release anger, he will likely sense this and direct force back toward you (probably much harder).

Lasting Motivation is Self-Motivation

Ultimately, you can't lastingly motivate others externally. Yet some people keep fighting this losing battle. They hire a "motivational speaker" who brings in lots of energy, but no concrete skills. They pass out inspiring books and constantly exhort staff to "win one for the Gipper." These strategies, while useful in their place, will not motivate anyone in the long run. All that happens is that staff become "hooked" on motivational excitement, but the effects are always short-lived.

Ruth Engle is a consumer loan centre supervisor in a bank who is painfully aware that her employer mistreats its workers. To offset this, she periodically uses creative tricks to keep morale high. Sometimes she holds draws where staff can win a day with an hour off. She also encourages potluck lunches and initiates staff holiday celebrations. These strategies somewhat soften the impact of heavy-handed upper management, but they don't change the reality. Employees feel good about their supervisor for trying, but they are still angry at their employer. This is reflected in their service to customers.

Don't try to motivate staff. It's like filling a cup with a hole in it. You have to keep pouring the motivation in because it leaks out almost as quickly. This is very tiring and inefficient. Besides, what happens when you are not around to fill the cup? Instead, plug the leak. Help employees motivate themselves.

In the martial arts, the easiest way to move people is first to make contact with them; then, join with their direction of movement; and finally, steer them to the desired course.

In a management context, making contact does not mean being your employees' friend; in fact, there are disadvantages to this. First, get close to them by sitting down and talking in a non-threatening location. Match their pace and tone of voice (unless they are really upset). Above all, really listen. Listening is not a passive skill; it is an active art that few people have mastered. Stay black-belt calm. Listen by really focusing on them and letting go of your own concerns for that moment. If you listen to your staff, they'll know you are concerned about them and will work doubly hard for you.

Second, match their emotional direction to understand how they see things. This doesn't mean you should be as angry or negative as they are, just see things from their perspective. Don't offer advice too quickly or judge their situation with thoughts like "if it were I, I wouldn't let myself be placed in that position to begin with."

Third, while maintaining contact with them, move yourself. Gradually, raise your own energy level and attitude. Slowly suggest ways you can remedy the situation. Most of the time, they will come along with you, feeling immediately more hopeful and calm. But how can you make this positive tone last? It has to be grounded in reality. Words are not enough. The original problem has to be overcome and their work really has to improve.

The literal meaning of "samurai" is "one who serves." The duty of the samurai was, at any moment, to give their all to the leader to whom they were pledged. The warrior dedicates his service to his lord or master; the accomplished manager focuses on serving his employees.

Follow the wisdom of Lao Tzu: "To lead the people, walk behind them." Knowing his own productivity is really the output of his department or organization, a black-belt manager leads by helping employees do their job.

When there is a staff problem, the black-belt manager does *not* immediately draw a sword to sever the employee from the ranks. Instead, he sees the problem as his own. What has he done to allow this? What can he do differently to help this employee perform? This approach especially applies when the performance of a previously able worker begins to dip below acceptability. Of course, there are times when the employee seems determined to self-destruct. But if the subordinate is valued, the wise manager will try everything in his considerable arsenal to get him back on track.

There are many methods for teaching martial arts techniques. Sometimes the traditional approaches—demonstrating the technique or analysing the component movements—don't work. One effective technique to use with people who aren't getting it, and who often feel foolish or frustrated at this point, is to move alongside them. To teach them how to parry a punch, literally stand behind them, pick up their hand, and deflect the incoming blow. Do this several times. At first, ask them to let you move their limbs, then direct them to concentrate on feeling your path of movement. Finally, have them parry under their own power, with you watching. It's amazing how fast even non-athletic students can pick up new techniques this way.

As a manager, work closely alongside employees with problems until they are back on an even keel. Once they're doing well, gradually pick up the work pace. In effect, you are teaching them how to walk by letting them lean on you for the first steps. Once they get the feeling of walking, they will depend on you less. They can, and will, motivate themselves to act effectively.

Motivating the Unmotivated: The Apathetic and the Dissident

The experienced martial artist would rather face a strongly rushing assailant than one who enters slowly. This form of attack may be less psychologically threatening (less speed is involved), but it is more difficult to counter. The physics of movement apply: "a body at rest tends to remain at rest; a body in motion tends to remain in motion." The more static the attack, the more balanced the opponent. In contrast, a highly energized assault tends to be less balanced and thus more easily diverted.

In the same way, an apathetic employee is harder to motivate than one who is vocally dissident. If people are unmotivated, they may really be resisting because they already feel pushed. As an initial strategy, back off so you don't strengthen any resistance they may have. Then search for areas where they are motivated. (For example, they are enthusiastic hikers.) Ask yourself, then them, what they get out of it. ("They love the feeling of being alone and free.") How can you harness this existing motivation at work? ("They would prefer a project where they can work autonomously.") Once you've got them moving, it's just a matter of steering them in the right direction, into alignment with the organization.

In contrast, the dissident employee is much more aggressive about expressing dissatisfaction. But it is possible to turn his charge to your ends. Don't think about fighting his natural tendencies; instead, plan channelling them toward a useful direction.

This kind of employee is already motivated, but is just not aligned with organizational goals. Meet with him; hear him out. Ask him if he would be interested in helping make things better by being a part of the solution. Enlist his perceptiveness and energy toward organizational goals. You may develop an excellent employee. One organization, frustrated with low productivity and morale, decided to promote only vocally disaffected employees to supervisory positions. With careful training and supervision, productivity and morale soon skyrocketed.

Customizing Supervision

You can't teach all martial arts students the same way. Beginners learn by imitating. They are shown exactly where to place their feet, and how to kick in stages. In contrast, intermediate students don't need this simplistic instruction. They are shown how to make their movements smooth and well-timed. Advanced students are learning how to develop their own techniques. They go beyond imitation to think through underlying principles they can adapt and use creatively. Walter Muryasz said that when students get their black belt, "their practice is their own; they are independent learners," able to progress without explicit supervision.

A national judo champion attended several jujitsu classes. He expected it to be easy, thinking that he'd be able to learn new movements the first time through. But is wasn't to be. He put so much pressure on himself, he couldn't learn. When he saw martial arts novices surpassing him in skill, he gave up in frustration. He couldn't take off his black belt mentally and become the white belt he truly was in a different form.

Similarly, it makes no sense in management to ignore employees' individual level. Trusting a new employee to make crucial decisions is not trust at all, it's naiveté. Instead, perceive the employee's true level, then help him grow to the next stage. If the task is new to him, he's a white belt. He may progress through the ranks quickly, becoming a purple-belt intermediate, then a black-belt expert. But the fastest way for him to get there is by being supervised according to his present level of expertise.

Not only do people learn this way; the job gets done well. Musashi was a proponent of this principle in 1645. In *The Book of Five Rings*, he wrote, "The Way of the foreman carpenter is the same as the Way of the commander of a warrior house. The foreman carpenter must know natural rules . . . . He allots his men work according to their ability.

Those of poor ability lay the floor joists, and those of lesser ability carve wedges and do such miscellaneous work. If the foreman knows and deploys his men well, the finished work will be good. The foreman should take into account the abilities and limitations of his men, circulating among them and asking nothing unreasonable. He should know their morale and spirit, and encourage them when necessary. This is the same as the principle of strategy."

Just as most martial masters are dedicated to teaching, black-belt managers enjoy helping their people grow. Ron Swingen believes his role as a manager is to help employees learn that "their power is inside themselves." He emphasizes training and cross-training people, and rotating them where appropriate. He helps them by customizing his supervision to their level of skill.

Whenever someone undertakes a new task, wrote Andrew Grove in *High Output Management*, he has a low level of maturity. It makes no difference if he was highly accomplished in his old job. The expert programmer promoted to supervisor, the engineer assigned to train others, or the salesman asked to add a new product to his line are all beginners at that time.

Here is the key. Match your style to each employee's task maturity level. If he's new at the task, a white belt with a low task maturity, treat him accordingly. Be directive and structured. Tell him specifically what to do, when and how to do it. If he wears the coloured belt of medium task maturity, employ his skills while helping him gain a black belt. This is the time to emphasize two-way communication. Make strategy together. Support him when he either fails or does especially well.

With mature black-belt staff, you can be minimally involved as a supervisor. Establishing and monitoring objectives should be sufficient. But remember, like that judo expert, when a black belt changes arts or tasks, he becomes a beginner once again, at least for a time.

In the martial arts, one need only look at a student's belt colour to get a *general* idea of how experienced and accomplished he is. But how can you gauge subordinates "belt rank" at work? Of course, notice the quality of their work; also watch how they get things done (frantically, at the last moment, or calmly paced?) Also watch how they move—in large, small, or "no" circles. Do they feel confident enough to listen well, ask questions, and request needed assistance?

Timing for Learning

One of the strengths of martial arts training is that is teaches people how to learn. The student discovers that learning requires commitment to a lifelong process of trial and error. There is never a point of "having totally arrived." In fact, certain throws are informally labelled a "twenty-five year technique," another a "lifetime technique." By keeping in mind that some skills can take a long time to acquire, you will be more realistic when helping others—and yourself—develop their skills.

There is a popular expression, "if you give a person a fish, he will eat for a meal. If you teach him how to fish, he will eat for a lifetime." The point is that continually bailing others out of their problems keeps them dependent and doesn't help them learn. But the aphorism can be taken too far. If a person is starving you can't teach her how to fish; she won't listen.

It is like taking seed corn to starving people, intending to teach them to farm. They will eat the seeds, not because they are backward, but because they are hungry. Feed them first; then, when the gnawing in their belly has quieted, teach them how to procure their own food.

Similarly, some managers lose their balance and go overboard. They make the mistake of treating everything as a chance to train staff. It's not a bad philosophy overall, but one that's sure to frustrate others if the timing is bad. When someone comes to you with a problem *he* considers important, show him you take it seriously. "Fill his stomach" by helping solve the problem. Then and only then look for ways to make the situation into a learning exercise.

ADJUSTING THE WORK CLIMATE

Musashi's nine guidelines in chapter one highlighted the importance of "trifles." The martial artist modifies his movements and strategies for different opponents and varying conditions. The adjustments are minute and may seem trifling, but they are absolutely essential. Techniques that are fine on an open street may be disastrous in a phone booth. What works against a tall, powerful opponent may not work with the small, fast adversary. With subtle adjustments, you can improve productivity and morale by tailoring the work place to fit the employee.

With the right tools and work place design techniques, it is possible to eliminate environment problems. Work place design techniques involve ergonomics, the science of energy and of work. The principle of ergonomics is to improve the fit between workers and their environment. Many people associate ergonomics with specially designed chairs for computerized offices. But ergonomics has far wider application than in expensive furniture.

Consider the whole environment. Make sure work stations are the right height for comfortable assembly or computing. Clearly, too much straining creates useless tension, will lower employees' productivity, and can cause disabling injuries.

Frequently used materials should be easily accessible. Furniture should comfortably fit the human body. The employees can use bent-handled tools to reduce wrist strain (preventing a condition known as carpal tunnel syndrome) and more efficiently transfer their power to their tasks. If you buy specially designed chairs or tools, be sure to train employees in their use. Otherwise you may be wasting your money; without the proper instruction, employees can still slump in an expensive chair.

Using Body Mechanics to Ease Work

You can train employees to use their bodies more efficiently. Motion analysis, pioneered by Frank Gilbreth at the beginning of the twentieth century, uses principles of body mechanics identical to those of the martial arts.

These principles can help your staff move more efficiently. The martial artist knows that thoughts, emotions, and bodily feeling are connected. Effective physical motivation can lead to emotional commitment and mental dedication. Training can energize what I call the "Organizational Critical Triangle":

- *Productivity* increases with less wasted motion, reduced fatigue and better controlled non-verbal communication.

- *Safety* is enhanced as balance and co-ordination improve.

- *Morale* improves as stress diminishes. There is more energy available from greater movement efficiency and less pain from poor body mechanics.

Training should always be upbeat, exciting, and practical. Motivate employees by selling them the benefits of this training. Don't force it on them by saying, "This will improve your productivity and safety." Instead, offer it: "How would you like to learn some methods you can practise on the job that will improve your performance in any sport or hobby and also help you feel less tired at the end of the day?"

A good way to increase staff self motivation is to teach them methods that increase their sense of self control and power. If you show them the following techniques (as well as the methods of physical leverage in chapter three), their internal power should rise—and so will your credibility.

- Warm up to your tasks. Develop a one-minute warmup that prepares the specific muscles to be used.

- Work with your elbows in front of your ribs.

- Cool down at the end of the day to reduce tension.

These principles will make you feel and seem stronger, more confident, and relaxed.

Job Redesign

Some "body types" seem more suited to certain martial arts. Judo, with its get-under-opponents'-centre-of-gravity throws and leg sweeps seems designed for those with shorter legs. Tae kwon do—most of whose techniques are kicks—seems to favour those with long, supple legs. But stockier people can become excellent tae kwon do practitioners, and taller artists can become strong judo-ka. But they may have to redesign some of the techniques they study to suit their types.

To improve the fit between employees and their jobs, consider job redesign. It can be difficult to find good people, and it is tougher still to keep them. It is often worth the expense to redesign jobs to make a good fit.

If you have a valued employee who has outgrown her duties, or just doesn't fit her department, try adjusting her duties to her skills, or switching her to another division. Remember to involve her—and both her old and new supervisors—in planning this change. Typically, employees' morale and performance will improve with such a move.

The positive effects from doing this are often broader; other staff who are aware of this redesign process will usually feel better about management as a result of your efforts.

You can also train promising people for new positions. In the martial arts, just about everyone can become a black belt with the right attitude. The same is true in the work place—if you find the right place for them.

Raising Low Morale

It is often the simple things that are effective. Everyday motions can become self-defence techniques, and managers can employ simple actions to boost worker morale and thereby improve the general atmosphere and climate.

Julie Hale noticed the people in her financial services department were becoming too stressed, so she instituted a "take a lap" program. Whenever she sees a staff member taking things too seriously or becoming too angry, Julie pulls her aside and smilingly says, "Enough is enough. Why don't you just take a lap?" And she expects this staff member to take a break (up to fifteen minutes), work things out, and come back feeling better. This works, probably because of the way Julie does it. She catches the problem before it becomes massive and uses humour and her "no-nonsense-you-can-do-it" attitude to support the person. After a time, her staff started telling peers in need to "take a lap." Department morale, and productivity, is extremely high, even though Julie's organization is in the midst of profound changes.

If you sense staff morale is low and you ask employees to voice their concerns, you have entered the realm of raw power. First, be prepared to be initially inundated with negative responses. These will always surface first. Second, control your reactions and hear them out, even if you begin to feel personally threatened. One of the worst things you can do is shut off expressions of anger or dissatisfaction after you have opened the way for expressing them.

After hearing employees out, it's crucial that you do something. Any time you ask staff to share their concerns, they assume you are making a tacit contract to do what you can to improve the situation. So, listen and thank them for their frankness and their interest in making the organization stronger and a better place to work. Then explain what you can and can't reasonably do to make things better. Give them specifics, what you'll attempt and when you'll get back to them. Then follow through. This is a high-leverage time. You will lose tremendous credibility if you don't take them seriously or let their concerns fall through the cracks. But if you follow through as promised, and improve some things, you can encourage tremendous loyalty.

The Loyalty Balance

In the *Tao Te Ching*, Lao Tsu writes, "Fail to honour people; they fail to honour you." It seems every manager wants loyalty. But many try to secure it the wrong way. Loyalty is a two-way street. Act loyally to your employees and they will be loyal to you. In an employment interview, asking prospective employees for a two-year commitment doesn't make sense—and prospective hires will know it—unless you, as an employer, are willing to give them the same promise. Try honestly to improve subordinates' work situation and they will be willing to go the extra mile on your projects.

Loyalty in an organization can be seriously undermined by gossip. The way to control gossip is to direct it, as a martial artist defends himself against a knife. Don't block it—it's too easy to make an error and get cut. And trying to shut off rumours usually has the opposite effect. Instead, think of the knife as your own weapon: direct it away from you and toward the attacker.

Bring things into the open. Secrecy not only excites more speculation, it also requires lots of energy to maintain. Ask people what they've heard. Tell them what you know: "We're watching this quarter's sales. And we don't know now if we will have any more layoffs. We'll tell you as soon as we know." The truth frequently makes rumours less enticing.

STRENGTHENING THE TEAM

It's important for the martial artist to tap his talents effectively when working with others, as well as when working alone. It has been said that "the code of conduct of the sixteenth-century samurai is summed up by the phrase 'for the team.' " But it is difficult for people to think in this way. Our training and culture go against this. Growing up, we are told, "You're unique and can be anything you want," not "you are part of a society and need to work with others." We deplore the idea of "groupthink," losing individuality, and merely going along with the crowd. So we have a work force of individuals, many of whom have difficulty working on projects with others, dread meetings, and quarrel when diverted from their personal goals. (Of course, on the other side, this system encourages *individual* creativity.)

But in this complex and changing world, no one person has all the information or answers. We need to pool our efforts to create what is beyond any individual's scope. Black-belt managers make it easier for their staff to work as a team.

Meetings are a good starting place. First, acknowledge why people resist meetings:

- Meetings use more collective time to perform a simple task than any individual would use.

- Participation in groups can be frustrating for those who don't get what they want.

- People may be forced to associate with colleagues they would rather avoid.

- Group work dissipates the glory any individual would have received for doing a good job.

- Committees can encourage controversy or conflict.

- Groups can make the simple, complex. Hence the expression "a camel is a horse designed by committee."

- Committees are frequently used to postpone work or to avoid facing a controversial problem. ("Let's delegate that to a committee.")

- Meetings can put individuals on the spot by pressuring them to state opinions publicly.

- Groups can lessen personal accountability for work.

- Group assignments can foster unequal workloads that are a fertile ground for resentment and lowered morale.

- Meetings are often just plain boring, especially for those who already know the material being covered, or for those who operate at a higher pace than others.

No wonder many employees' feelings about committees or other work groups are negative. And frequently, staff expect future groups to be similarly ineffective or boring. But this doesn't have to be.

On the other side, "teamthink" can be extremely effective. It can

- Increase creativity. While follow-the-leader "groupthink" leads to narrow-mindedness and tunnel vision, a team approach synergizes thought. Participants stimulate one another, so that the whole becomes far greater than the sum of the parts.

- Reduce resistance to change by encouraging those who implement a program to feel allegiance to it. A good way to invite commitment is to ask for involvement in the planning of any project.

- Spread workload so that more gets done.

- Improve planning. A critical group, with numerous viewpoints, is less likely to miss an important contingency than is a person working alone.

- Foster more satisfying work relationships, as people get to work in a positive, productive manner with peers.

How can you sharpen work group effectiveness?

- Provide training in group dynamics to make any team more efficient.

- Rotate leadership so everyone has the fun—and frustration—of keeping the meeting on track.

- Encourage members to do their homework in advance by completing subcommittee assignments, reading meeting minutes, and thinking through the objectives of the next meeting. Meeting time can then be dedicated to exploring ideas and making decisions, instead of rehashing old business or arguing about easily verifiable information. Nothing is more frustrating than an ineffective meeting, *and* leaves a sour taste about team projects.

- Start off all meetings by reminding participants of the meeting's purpose. Review the goals and objectives of your team. Read the organization's mission statement. Have a prepared agenda.

- Call off unnecessary meetings. Ask yourself whether a memo can accomplish the same purpose.

- Shorten all meetings. A good rule of thumb is to limit informational meetings to forty-five minutes and decision-making meetings to ninety minutes.

Making meetings more efficient and enjoyable will change the bad image of work groups. Staff will look forward to well-run meetings that increase their creativity, productivity, and social interaction.

By understanding why people resist and how to enlist the mechanics of softness and hardness, you can build stronger, more dedicated staff. You will also strengthen your managerial power and control.

Motivating Through Softness and Hardness: Techniques for Action

- Notice your reactions to being pushed or forced. Can you observe these feelings without reacting?

- Reinterpret the meaning of "soft." Think of the synonyms flexible, malleable, adaptable, supple, yielding, lenient, limber, and resilient.

- Critically assess your past motivational style and that of your organization. What has worked and why? How much of this motivation is based on "supercharging" or on making subordinates uncomfortable?

- Look for new ways of inviting, rather than controlling others. Think of controls that are unnecessary and could be given up without adverse effect on productivity.

- Use secondary pressure to reach an "unreachable" person. Notice when indirect strategies will take you closer to your goals.

- Encourage employees to become self-motivated rather than trying to motivate them externally.

- Practise making real contact with others. Look for the subtle feeling that you are "in contact."

- Practise seeing things as others see them.

- Look for cost-effective adjustments you can make to the workplace; solicit employees' ideas on this.

- Practise motion efficiency.

- Develop a customized supervision plan for each of your subordinates. Start by asking yourself, "what is each one's belt colour?" (level of task maturity)

- Train all staff in group leadership and meeting skills.

- Give them a fish, *then* teach them how to fish.

- Give as much loyalty as you ask from your staff.

- Ask yourself "How else can I strengthen my employees?"

CHAPTER SIX

The Martial Art of Conflict

There is no opponent or enemy in true budo. *True* budo *is at one with the universe which means being united with the centre of the universe. True* budo *is a labour of love. It involves giving life to all that exists and not killing or opposing one another.*

Morehei Ueshiba, *Aikido*

Men are your castles
Men are your walls
Sympathy is your ally
Enmity your foe.

Takeda Shingen, sixteenth century warrior

Budo, "The Way of the martial arts," in more literal Japanese means "to control the conflict." In his *Ideals of the Samurai: Writings of Japanese Warriors*, William Scott Wilson quotes the Chinese source Tso Chuan: "*Bu* means stopping the spear. *Bu* prohibits violence and subdues weapons . . . it puts people at peace, and harmonizes the masses." As might be expected, over the centuries the martial arts have developed powerful strategies and techniques for managing conflict.

In feudal Japan, the sword was commonly said to be the "soul of the samurai." Two sword makers, Masamune and Muramasa, were both known for making excellent blades, strong and sharp and not easily broken. But Muramasa was known to be a lover of war. It was said those who owned his blades went mad with violence. Legend has it that one could tell the difference between Masamune and Muramasa swords by placing the blades in a stream. Leaves would bypass the former, but would be attracted to and cleaved in two by the latter. Although both were excellent pieces of workmanship, Masamune blades became highly prized while Muramasa's were shunned.

Traditional martial artists were proponents of peace. The most valued warriors were those who could have a calm, peaceful outlook even during a conflagration. Hojo Soun is quoted in *The Ideals of the Samurai*: "There is a saying that goes 'Even though one associates with many people, he should never cause discord.' In all things one should support others." The martial artist viewed conflict as a natural part of life, but he also developed a wide range of methods of control to make conflict work for him.

Like martial artists, managers get ample exposure to conflict. Most managers I have surveyed believe there is more conflict now than there was twenty years ago. Increases in stress, the rate of change, and competition for market share and resources have increased conflicts. A recent American Management Association study revealed that corporate executives and managers spend from eighteen to fifty percent of their time dealing with conflict, depending on their level and type of organization. Hospital administrators, public sector managers, and school administrators allocate the most time to managing conflict.

The ability to manage conflict has become increasingly important. Poorly managed conflict diverts energy from productivity, obstructs co-operative action, and fosters a climate of suspicion and mistrust. Conflict doesn't have to be your enemy. By applying martial arts methods, you can become a more skilled and confident manager of conflict, and learn how to use its inherent energy to your advantage.

THE CONFLICT PRINCIPLE

There are always people ready to push on you, whether they are customers demanding special treatment, subordinates acting sullenly obstinate when you delegate tasks to them, bosses setting unreasonable expectations without providing adequate support, highway tailgaters demanding you get out of their path, or children probing for your weak spots and insecurities. With any of these examples, the result is usually conflict, even if the symptoms are subtle, because when people feel pushed, they push back. Or they dig in their heels. They give in to your authority grudgingly, hide behind their job description, or do things as slowly as possible, and even miss work.

Non-verbal communication is a major source of "pushing." Communication experts say over ninety percent of all communication is non-verbal, consisting of the way something is said: tone and loudness of voice, speed of speech, and body movement. Non-verbal "pushes" can be as subtle as abruptly making an assignment without first saying hello, throwing papers at someone ("Please get this done as soon as possible!"), not respecting someone's distance, conversing too closely for comfort, or hovering over an employee's shoulder.

Most conflict management strategies for the work place focus on verbal communication; that is, we should say this, repeat that, or negotiate so. I won't repeat these here. Although verbal communication techniques can be effective in conflicts that involve facts and methods, the most difficult conflicts are emotional, involving goals and values; they don't lend themselves to intellectual and purely verbal solutions. In non-verbal communication people read actions, not words.

The Art of Japanese Management presents a study that reveals what most people know by common sense: when there is stress in an organization, people cease believing what is said and give more credence to how messages are given. Actions speak louder than words.

The manager's task is to control conflict and to direct it. Having mastered these skills, the manager will accomplish more and strengthen his organization. These skills also apply to his personal and family relationships.

ORGANIZATIONAL HARMONY AND CONFLICT

Martial artists ultimately strive for harmony. Real harmony is vibrant! It is a vital state. Nature continually demonstrates that great stability exists only in the midst of movement, as in the eye of the hurricane or the centre of a gyroscope. Stay in the centre of the circle of attack, many martial arts teach. Move so your opponent circles around you. Let things swirl outwardly; just keep your core calm.

A harmonious work place is marked by high efficiency, strong morale, and creative use of conflict, and by a staff that feels interdependent. ("If you do well, we all do well. If the company goes belly-up, we all suffer.") Harmony is not characterized by symptoms of stagnancy, boredom or low productivity, or by the signs of fear, sycophantic agreement ("yes-men"). In organizations with such symptoms, harmony exists only on the surface. The organizational reality underneath seethes with a low level of vitality, individual depression, and anger.

In the harmonious organization, competition, both internal and in the marketplace, is not seen as a lurking menace, but as a force that strengthens the company. In an excellent book about learning, *The Inner Game of Tennis*, Tim Gallwey observes that good competition challenges people to stretch beyond their present limits. The result, he suggests, will be higher performance.

Unfortunately, many organizations try to preserve an illusion of control and placidity. Grumbling and dissatisfaction are pushed below the surface, and erode organizational strength from within. A climate of fear is created—fear of ruthless internal competition, of overcontrol by management, and of retribution. Employees know what to avoid and how to appear busy. They spend more energy on covering themselves than on doing the job or trying new approaches to their work.

In the harmonious organization, on the other hand, disagreement does not have to lead to discord. When people feel confident and safe in expressing their opinions and when the focus is on team achievement rather than on self-serving actions, dissension can further productivity. For example, the power of brainstorming springs from an emphasis on group achievement and from ground rules that protect people from personal criticism. Without conflict, there is no creativity; controlled conflict drives new ideas and approaches. Good conflicts are also learning experiences.

There are specific policies that lead to more true harmony in an organization. Rules—which usually cause resistance—are kept to a minimum, so as to concentrate on crucial matters such as pursuit of the mission, organizational survival, or worker safety. Policy and procedure manuals are also thin, and are based on common sense. (People rarely read or use them for day-to-day functioning anyway.) The best-accepted policies are those developed with employee and managerial input. Once procedures are formulated, it's best that everyone concerned receives training.

Employees are treated as adults. People resent being patronized or treated like children. Conflicts are recognized early, when small, and dealt with. Feedback is regularly solicited and unhappy workers are encouraged to reveal the causes of their dissatisfaction. Managers sincerely respond to employee concerns.

Not just managers and supervisors, but all employees are expected to be conflict management specialists. Staff are trained to intervene appropriately when peers need help. The harmony that results from these policies assures that less harmful conflicts occur. When they do rear up, conflicts are more susceptible to resolution before they reach a dangerous level of energy.

CONTROLLING CONFLICT BY CONTROLLING YOURSELF

The strongest martial artists go out of their way to avoid a physical confrontation; they have nothing to prove. Author Terry Dobson tells a story about when he was an intermediate martial arts student. He wanted to prove his strength to the world. One day, while riding a train, he saw a drunk accost a group of people. Just as Terry got ready to do physical battle, a martial arts master quietly intervened. He calmly spoke to the drunk, who, ashamed of his actions, fell to his knees and cried. The threat was over; no blows were needed. Terry says he learned more about the martial arts, and himself, from this one incident than from years of training hall practice.

All kinds of people practice the martial arts, and there are those who do because they like to fight. Usually, as they mature in their practice, this fighting nature withers.

Martial artists experience the emotions of conflict. Being attacked, even in sparring, can elicit fear, anger, aggression, and frustration. In anyone, these emotions can provoke over-reaction. Controlling conflict begins with controlling yourself.

Master Shiba Yoshimasa's famous advice to developing samurai is quoted in *Ideals of the Samurai*: "There is nothing more base than for a man to lose his temper too often. No matter how angry one becomes, his first thought should be to pacify his mind and come to a clear understanding of the situation at hand. Then, if he is in the right, to become angry is correct.

"Becoming angry simply on account of one's own bias is unreasonable, and one will not be held in respect. Thus, though one may become more and more angry, there will be no result. It is reason alone by which people feel humbled and for which they feel respect."

How do martial arts experts successfully control their emotions when under attack? Master Don Angier advises his students in yanagi-ryu not to get emotionally involved when attacked. This is easy to say, he tells them, but achieving such detachment requires much work.

Martial artist and manager both should be able to recognize the dynamics of conflict, to see their own attitudes and feelings honestly, and to develop skills to influence conflict situations. They learn that conflict is not the enemy; in fact, it can be skilfully directed toward the greater good. Terry Dobson tells his students that when he is attacked, it is a "gift of energy wrapped in violence. I simply accept the energy without the package."

Successfully managing the energy of conflict requires taking control of fear. This is a real problem for many of the managers I've worked with. People are often hampered by fears of rejection, losing status, or appearing ignorant. They may also be afraid of retribution by their peers or superiors. ("What will she do to me when my back is turned?") Still others fear losing control or appearing to be afraid; they often compensate for their fear with over-aggressiveness. ("How dare they object? I'll show them!") Though they are continually demonstrating their "courage," fear controls them.

Some managers have trouble managing conflict because they fear new problems. ("Better not bring that up. It might mushroom and blow us all up.") Some fear that speaking honestly will cost them their jobs. Many of these managers don't believe they can control themselves if push comes to shove. ("What if I just explode?") Others are concerned their superiors will over-react.

People fear physical retaliation. Unfortunately, they have some reason. Statistics reveal that physical attacks directed at co-workers or supervisors are on the rise, with employees in frequent contact with the public being especially at risk. Even when actual physical attacks don't occur, the resulting undercurrent of intimidation drains energy from strong performance. How can a fearful manager enact unpopular measures? Whatever the fear involved, it can harm job performance and prevent a manager from dealing decisively with conflict.

Fear aside, any rigid management style may disable a manager from successfully working with conflict. Martial artists know that a person's strength will also be his weakness. A strong kicker may rely too much on his foot strength; a good thrower may always try to close distance, even when it's not appropriate. Any one style has a narrow application.

In the same vein, a manager with a set management style (for example, he always tries to smooth out any signs of conflict) will only be effective within a narrow range of conflicts. The desire to smooth conflicts can play into the hands of someone who refuses to be quietly mollified and threatens to make a scene. A one-style manager may be stymied if the situation calls for a different approach.

Making Conflict an Ally

Martial artists employ the physical laws of energy and mass to maximize the power in strikes and throws. Conflict is a form of energy, which, as Einstein's Law of Conservation of Energy shows, cannot be created or destroyed. But it can be channelled toward productivity or other corporate goals. Organizational dynamics expert Gordon Lippitt agrees: "Conflict releases energy at every level of human affairs, energy that can produce positive, constructive results. . . . The goal is not to eliminate conflict, but to use it, to turn the released energy to good advantage."

Because managers are problem-solvers, conflicts in an organization fall squarely under their responsibility. Also, the managerial role is basically an aggressive one. Their job is to help others (employees) *change*, become more efficient, work better together, and align themselves with organizational goals, all of which are potential sources of conflict.

Through strong conflict management, managers influence where and how organizational energy is directed. For instance, conflict can be exciting enough to wake up a sleeping department or organization. And conflict is the parent of creativity. When people are satisfied with the status quo, and everything runs smoothly, there is no creativity. Conflicting values, opinions, and ideas spur the development and trial of new, more efficient methods.

Just as sparring partners feel the harmony of comradeship after a good workout, an organization which has a healthy approach to conflict can achieve true harmony. Once people express their objections and thrash out a difficult problem, the groundwork has been laid for calm problem-solving.

Well-managed conflict also

- brings alternate sides of issues to the surface;
- clarifies an issue by letting people air and work out their objections;
- increases participation and involvement;
- improves the quality of problem-solving;

- makes communication easier;

- strengthens relationships;

- enlivens and renews an organization;

- is a powerful training aid, providing an example to employees of how unexpected "people problems" can be realistically handled;

- helps an organization clean house of excess emotional "baggage"; and

- fosters organizational, professional, and personal growth.

Conflict is truly not your enemy. By learning to see its dynamics like a martial artist, you will learn to harness it to positive ends.

Conflict is Blind

Unfortunately, conflict often blinds the combatants. Walter Muryasz asks a partner to push her fist strongly against his. Mr. Muryasz then places his other fist on top of her hand and takes away his original hand. Almost always his partner immediately pushes against the second hand. Whereas she was first pushing forward, she is now pushing up *without being aware of the switch*. When people are in a forceful frame of mind, they seek conflict everywhere. They push and look for a push back.

Mr. Muryasz has mastered this principle to throw opponents. He manœuvres to push against then so that they will exert their force toward a direction of imbalance—they are, in effect, heavily leaning on him; at that point, Mr. Muryasz merely removes his support and they fall.

So people will follow perceived or real resistance, wherever it leads. Once involved in conflict, most people cannot see what they're doing. They become ineffective when dealing with colleagues or making important decisions. Emotions cloud reason. Even brilliant managers may do something that is potentially unfixable.

Conflict is blind in another way. When people are in a conflictive frame of mind, they generally cannot see that they share the fault. Ask any two warring parties what has happened and you'll hear each say he believes the other is mostly to blame ("I wasn't doing anything; he came up to me and went crazy"). Most importantly, neither side sees that he may have escalated the conflict by pushing back *just a little bit harder*.

Of course, all of us try to push back where and when it is safe. If it is too risky to respond directly when pushed upon, there are numerous ways to push back indirectly, such as

- working only when we believe we are being monitored;

- passing the conflict on to others by mistreating our subordinates, peers, vendors, and customers;

- criticizing our boss and the organization;

- leaving for other employment;

- stealing from the organization; or

- sabotaging.

If you find yourself slipping into anger, calm yourself. Watching for the symptoms of hidden conflict can prevent it from blind-siding you. The seven warning signals of negative conflicts are

1. changes in relationships from helpful/supportive to hindering/resistive;
2. emotional wounds that don't heal;
3. unusual emotional outbursts or preoccupations (dwelling on past incidents) that continue;
4. persistent resistance to change;
5. a climate of anger or fear;
6. aggression or looking for fights;
7. difficulty making decisions or getting work done.

More than one of these signs is usually present before there is a serious conflict problem, but even a single symptom is worth investigation, simply because conflicts are generally easier to solve when dealt with early.

Although conflict is an emotional issue, almost anyone, no matter the age, size, sex, or position, can learn to manage conflict successfully—not just to squelch it, but to take advantage of it. Acknowledge that conflict is normal—it does not have to cause overwhelming shame or fear. The three-step approach to managing conflict is this:

- recognize the kind and level of conflict;

- decide what action to take;

• act, using martial arts-based conflict management techniques and strategies. These last two steps are closely related, so they'll be considered in the same section.

RECOGNIZING THE CONFLICT

The martial artist sees the conflict as an energetic process—nothing more than a cycle of building, releasing, and lowering of energy that is potentially useful to him. He must recognize and assess conflict because it determines how he will react.

Conflict means "to strike together." It happens between two or more people. If you don't push back, there is no real conflict. Push back, consciously or inadvertently, and energy increases. The conflict escalates, proceeding along its course. Conflict usually becomes personal only when we make it so.

The process of conflict is illustrated in the accompanying figure. First, energy builds. The signs are quite noticeable. Watch the non-verbal cues—the way the message is delivered. Voices rise or speed up, actions become more aggressive or faster, shoulders rise, blood rushes to the face, eye contact becomes more intense, and responses are overly forceful.

When people are highly charged, near the top of their conflict curve, they can't be reasonable; don't expect it of them. Solutions aren't appreciated, even those that seem to solve the problem. So this isn't the time to be logical with them. Not only is it difficult to get those in conflict to consider that there is a solution, there can be resistance and over-identification with issues ("Are you suggesting there's something wrong with my project?"), as well as a lack of appropriate caution, and jockeying for power. Should you jump in (and who hasn't), you will likely hear: "Yes, but . . . ," or "I tried that . . . ," or "You don't understand. . . ." You'll see that their energy level doesn't lower; it may even rise. You're actually reinforcing the conflict.

At some point, which varies according to the situation involved, the energy in the conflict peaks and releases. Releases may be of varying sorts—screaming, crying, stomping away, slamming doors, throwing things, or even physical attacks. Then, after the release, there is a phase when energy lowers, the calm after the storm. People, at this point, because they have let go of emotions and energy that was clouding their vision, are usually more open-minded and approachable, unless some-

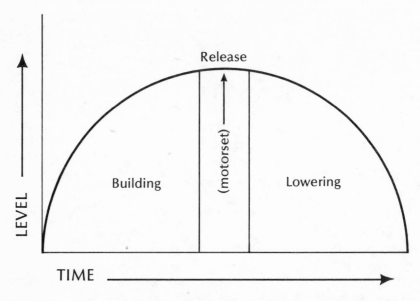

Figure 1. The Conflict Continuum

thing was said or done that had lasting repercussions and that they'd wind up dwelling on.

Just before someone releases energy, there is usually a point where nothing happens, a point of free fall. It's like the moment at the height of a jump when you are momentarily suspended, neither rising nor falling. This is a critical moment. At the peak of the conflict curve, someone can go either toward explosion or to calmness. Walter Muryasz calls this point "motorset." Muscles are braced for action and yet held in check, as if they were simultaneously stopped and waiting for a command to "Go." Motorset is the moment of thick tension when "you can hear a pin drop," the suspenseful second when everything is on the verge of releasing.

In motorset the mind has given the body contingency instructions: "If this happens, you will immediately react." Mr. Muryasz says motorset is fairly common, even in everyday situations. Have you ever waited for a traffic light to turn green? The green arrow comes on and you involuntarily start to go? If so, you have experienced motorset. Your mind had commanded your body, "Go on the green." Even though you received the "wrong" stimulus—an arrow instead of the light changing—you still reacted.

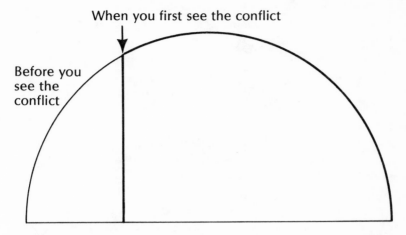

Figure 2. Your Initial View of the Conflict

It's important to be able to recognize when people are motorset. If you do not want them to explode, don't do anything. Even a conciliatory gesture can push them over the edge. If you wish to help them become calmer, take control by doing nothing to them. Relax yourself, breathe, and control your own attitude. Motorset is a state of high tension that takes a large expenditure of energy to maintain. Shortly, if not pushed over the edge, a person's motorset energy will relax, bypassing the most dangerous moment.

Recognizing when a person is at motorset isn't always easy. When you encounter an angry person, his level of anger may not have mounted before your eyes. The conflict may have had a long history, so that by the time he reaches you, he was already close to motorset. Make it a practice to approach upset people carefully and look for signs of motorset. When you discover their position on the conflict continuum, you will be able to deal with them more effectively.

Individuals react to conflict differently and reach motorset at their own rate. Working closely with someone enables you to note their conflict style. Recognizing their individual speed of building a conflict curve will allow you to intervene adeptly to make conflict work for you. Some people are "slow burners"; generally, their energy rises and releases slowly; they can tend to hold onto grudges for longer periods. In contrast, others have a "short fuse"; they are more explosive; their energy builds and releases quickly. They often are able to "forgive

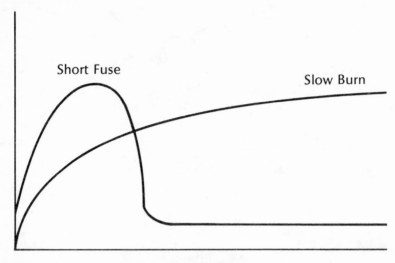

Figure 3. Different Conflict Styles

and forget" once their anger is released. Some people are a combination of the two.

Although you may know the people involved, read the conflict situation like a martial artist. Look beyond facial expressions—most people are somewhat adept at making masks—and concentrate on their entire bodies. Watch their hands.

Knowing *when* to say something can make the difference between heightened conflict (and wasted time) and profitable problem-solving. Like a martial artist, wait for the "suki," the opening. This opening comes as the conflict curve drops, past the point of motorset. Things are more calm and reasonable—this is the right moment to intervene. So when an upset person is no longer speaking and has wound down, the energy level is lower, and he or she will be more calm and receptive. This is the time to give your advice or make your suggestion.

CHOOSING AND ACTING ON A STRATEGY

Dealing with Threat and Intimidation: Fuelling

In the martial arts one learns that conflict has many guises, from angry glances, to manœuvring for position, to outright fighting. At work, conflict may be expressed as intimidation, threats, confrontation, back-stabbing, shunning, and harassment (including sexual).

Among the most direct and personally distressing forms of conflict are intimidation or threats, the weapons of a bully. Bullies are people who continually push others, with the hope of drawing a response, a push-back. Intimidation and threats are like an extended motorset. The bully maintains a conflict curve close to the point of release; the tension and energy are held at a constant, high level, without being released. The message is "I am right on the edge. If you do (or don't do) this or that, I will explode/quit/fire you/never speak with you again/take retribution." Most bullies are extremely sensitive. When they sense you pushing back, they know they "got to you." You cannot pretend to ignore or humour an intimidator when you're distressed, because the non-verbal signals are obvious to someone who is looking for them.

Sustaining intimidation requires a great expenditure of energy. Leaking out discomfort while trying to ignore the bully only strengthens him. To reduce intimidation, don't play into it. Make the bully carry the entire weight of the conflict on his or her own. There's a good chance he or she will tire and look for an easier target. Again, being able not to react to intimidation is easier said than done.

Paul Watzlawick offers a useful way to deal with threat and intimidation. In *How Real Is Real: Confusion, Disinformation, and Communication*, he presents the three conditions of successful threat:

1. It must be convincing or believable enough to be taken seriously.
2. It must reach its target—the threatened party.
3. The target must be capable of complying with it.

To neutralize a threat, he suggests, eliminate or disable one of the three conditions. For example, if you're able, you might make an even more serious counterthreat: "If you do that, company regulations require that I fire you; I'll have no choice." Or to prevent the threat reaching its target, you can put yourself out of the intimidator's reach. Last, you can show that you don't have the power to comply with the demand: "I'm sorry, I would like to help, but that is not within my role. You will have to speak with our Vice-President of Human Resources."

These are useful strategies, but I prefer also to consider the martial arts approach of changing the conflict curve. In other words, call the bluff. The intimidation plays on the fear caused by anticipation of the

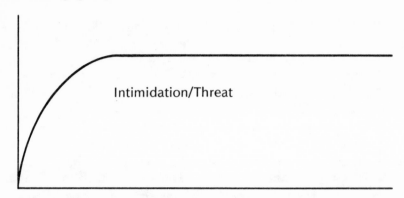

Intimidation/Threat

Figure 4. Intimidation is conflict energy sustained just below the point of release.

unknown (see chapter two). An unknown threat is usually more fright-ening than a known punishment.

Calling the bluff and bringing it out into the open where you can deal with it is much less frightening than projecting catastrophe about an unknown result.

Some fires smoulder invisibly, ever ready to flare up. Fire protection professionals may throw fuel on such a fire to make it flare up. When it is visible, the fire can be put out. Or starting their own "backfire" can control the blaze by eliminating fuel that's needed to spread. The strategy of *consciously* pushing with a strategic purpose is called Fuelling or Accelerating.

If you can't easily avoid an intimidator, and team performance is adversely affected, pick your time and place and confront the intimi-dator. By choosing the setting, you have made the first step toward controlling the conflict. In selecting the spot, ask yourself, do you want it to be more comfortable for him or for you? Is it better to have a group of supporters or neutral parties around, making it harder for him to deny what many others have seen, or is it better to be alone, so no one else sees what may transpire? Is it preferable to meet in your office, in his, or in some quiet restaurant? Sometimes the experienced conflict manager will choose the bully's favourite spot. There, he's likely to be less defensive and even slightly disarmed by your selection and timing.

Clearly, you will be more effective if you remain calm and relaxed. Practise some of the attitude and calming techniques in the first section of this book. In the fourteenth century, famed samurai Shiba Yoshimasa wrote (as quoted in Wilson's *Ideals of the Samurai*), "The man

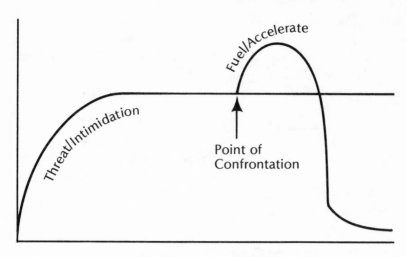

Figure 5. Confronting Intimidation or Conflict

whose profession is arms should calm his mind and look into the depths of others. Doing so is the best of the martial arts."

It's understandable if you feel angry toward your opponent. But you can be angry *and* calm. When people are angry and out of control, they have little credibility, even when they are speaking the truth. If you don't fight your emotions, you will be more relaxed and communicate with more clarity and power.

Be prepared for an emotional outburst from your opponent. Remember that there's a lot of energy wrapped up in intimidation, and your strategy here is to add fuel to the fire to bring the situation to a head (and eventually resolve it). Confront the person until he cannot deny what is happening—don't let him escape. Lancing this boil can speed the ultimate healing time, saving longer-term discomfort.

Sometimes, an antagonist will bad-mouth you to others, yet refuse to acknowledge there is any problem to your face. Fueling can bring behind-the-back talk to the surface. When people avoid resolving an ongoing conflict, they usually wind up sustaining a cold war. A manager can carefully fan the embers to force recognition of the conflict and to acknowledge there is any problem to your face. Fuelling can bring enough—you still have to resolve the underlying problem ("You have always seemed to give preferential treatment to others"). So, after the release process begins, follow through until the conflict curve lowers and the situation becomes safer.

If you choose a "fuelling" strategy, always bear in mind that accelerating conflict is dangerous. If you're not careful, fuelling glowing sparks can result in your being burned by a raging fire. Most of all, be careful not to lose control and throw fuel on the fire without careful planning. Fuelling is not a good thing to attempt when you're in an out-of-control rage.

But in spite of the risks, there are times when no other strategy will work and the risk is worth the probable gain. It's certainly worth trying when you feel disabled by intimidation or working in fear. In any case, it is important to remember that fuelling is only the *first* step; once problems are brought out into the open, the work of problem solving and negotiating begins.

Defusing: Mediating Conflicts

More often than not, it is better to reduce the conflict and safely channel the force away before it escalates dangerously. This is like throwing water on the fire, and I call it "defusing." Because defusing can require more time than other strategies it usually makes most sense when

- Conflict affects continuing relationships or long-term harmony.

- It is more important to win the war than the battle.

- Customers are adversely involved (even indirectly).

- Time is available, i.e., there's no emergency.

If you decide to defuse a conflict, it's best to act at an early stage; here, less effort will be required. At a higher energy level, fear and anger can freeze people into ridiculous, self-defeating stances, "cutting off their nose to spite their face," and the situation is more explosive. At such levels, it's necessary not to do anything that could be interpreted as personally threatening if you want to help the other person calm down.

In the martial arts, it's easier to defend yourself than to protect a third party. When the assault is not directed at you, it's more difficult to lead the attacker (as a bullfighter does with his cape) because he's not as easily influenced by your movements. And once you enter the fray, running

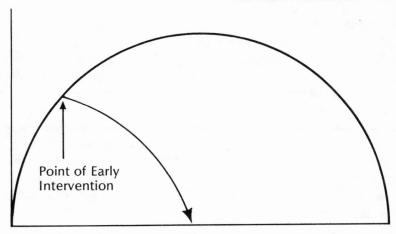

Figure 6. Defusing or "Throwing Water" on Conflict

away is no longer a good option; now you have to think of protecting not only yourself, but at least one and perhaps both combatants.

The problems of "third party mediation" are many: it is like a physical assault, more difficult to control than conflict directed at yourself; how can you help others deal with their own conflicts without taking their problems on yourself? When is it right to intervene and when to stay out? Generally, it's best not to get involved unless

- The conflicting parties have historically been unable to reach an accord.
- The conflict is adversely affecting others.
- The parties are at an impasse.
- They both request your intervention.

An interesting approach was suggested in a seminar by organizational dynamics expert Gordon Lippitt: "Look at the issues involved coldly and at the people involved warmly." This is akin to the martial artist's goal of staying unruffled during a fight while cleaving to the spirit of protection.

Keep your own long-term goals in mind. Are you trying to help these two to work harmoniously? Or do you perhaps want each to individually do his job? Or are you just hoping to keep them off your back? Design your mediation to achieve your goals.

Listening is one good way to safely channel away the force of conflict—really listening, not just going through the motions of repeating what the other person says, or of saying "uh-huh" every thirty seconds.

How can you judge the effectiveness of your conflict strategy? Watch the level of energy. In defusing the energy should lower—voices quieten, tensions decrease. If you're not seeing the results you want, try something different. It makes no sense to persist blindly with a strategy that doesn't help, like the beginning jujitsu student doggedly trying to apply a wristhold to an extremely flexible attacker. While there really is no way to know beforehand what will work, with experience you will tend to select more effective techniques. The following third-party mediation strategies may work.

Use a "separate/together sandwich." Interview each party individually and take notes of what they say. Be especially watchful for any acknowledgement of partial responsibility, as opposed to a purely "it's her fault" stance. Usually, by the time conflicts reach the manager for mediation, both parties are highly defensive and afraid they will be found in the wrong and lose status, advancement opportunities, or even their position. In these individual meetings, help calm them down and reduce defensiveness. Next, meet with them together. Control the tone. Show them that you don't want to assess blame, but to get things working well again.

If you choose to have a joint meeting, you can impose some rules, as a famous master once did. In *Ideals of the Samurai: Writings of Japanese Warriors,* William Scott Wilson writes "Both Kuroda Nagamasa (a seventeenth-century lord) and his father Josui were well known for their regard of others, and Nagamasa even set aside one night a month when he would sit with a number of his trusted retainers and allow all to talk freely with the mutual promise that none would become angry over what was said, or gossip about it later. These were called the 'Meetings Without Anger.' "

In a meeting with two opposing parties, it is best to accentuate their similarities: "I am pleased both of you are concerned with important details and that you want the division to seek out new directions." Consider assigning the two parties to a short-term project together. Suggest peaceful coexistence. Sometimes only a non-threatening invitation is necessary to break a stalemate. Ask for their help: "This conflict is dividing our department. Frankly, things are in a crunch. I need both of you to help." Adjust your style to the situation. You may be more or less authoritarian; this is useful when there is little time to resolve the issues and a quick solution is needed; when the conflict is a long-standing one that both parties express little hope of solving on their own; or when the conflict has been sharp or bitter *from the beginning*.

A less authoritarian style works best when both parties have cooled down and each has strong enough communication skills to work it out. Bear in mind their expectations of you as a mediator. At the beginning of a mediation, match their expectations of you. Don't start by being democratic if they're expecting you to smash through their problems with an iron fist. You can ease off or change your style later. Ultimately, however, the more they see the solution as their own, rather than imposed by you, the better and the more lasting the resolution.

The greater your credibility as a mediator, the more successful the intervention is likely to be. When you're highly skilled at managing conflict, people will note this and accord you the kind of respect that will make your job as mediator even easier in the future.

Enlist other agents. There may be others in the organization—peers of the conflicting parties or human resource specialists—who can also serve as mediators.

Train the antagonists in conflict management and mediation techniques. Now that you've given them a fish, teach them to fish. After the conflict has been successfully resolved, make use of it. Soon afterwards, discuss with the former antagonists what they learned from conflict and any lasting advantages they see from it: "That worked out nicely. How would you like to be able to head off these problems in the future?" or "You worked that through very well, albeit with some help. Would you be interested in learning how to help others, as I did with you?" You are modelling effective actions that others can use to improve their conflict management skills without depending on you. Deputizing them this way is a high leverage activity; it influences others over an extended time. In the future, they can become a force for improved conflict utilization within their own work areas.

Remember that mediation is not the only third-party strategy. You can also choose to separate the parties, support the underdog, or fire either or both. Generally, however, these strategies contribute to an appearance, not the reality, of harmony.

Avoiding or Displacing

Sometimes, even for a skilled warrior, retreat makes sense. In an often-related story, Miyamoto Musashi, while aboard a ferry, was challenged by a young warrior eager to gain a reputation. Seeing that the youth would not be mollified, Musashi reluctantly agreed. But he pointed out that fighting on the boat might result in injury to innocent people. So he suggested that the two of them take the ferry's small lifeboat to a nearby island. The youth eagerly agreed. Musashi beckoned the young warrior to enter the rowboat first, implying that he would follow. But once his young challenger was aboard, Musashi cast off the boat's line. Without oars, the youth could only float helplessly away as Musashi calmly looked on.

Avoiding or displacing is a conflict strategy that moves the conflict energy safely away, either by moving you from it, or by moving it from you. This is a common strategy, probably because many people are uncomfortable or unskilled in conflict situations; also, avoiding is relatively easy to do. Common examples of displacing are

- *firing* a problem employee
- *humouring* or *ignoring* a chronically negative person (who, everyone agrees, "should have been terminated long ago and can't be fired now")
- *separating* feuding people: ("Why don't we change their shifts, or even move them to different areas of the building?")
- *withdrawing* from conflict ("I see that's a problem, but I really have to go now.")
- *passing a conflict on* ("Someone else can better help you with this.")

The problem with avoiding is that it doesn't lower the conflict energy, or solve the problem. It merely moves it out of sight, and out of mind. As an example, schools use displacement extensively when they suspend, expel, or remove students to detention. But the anger, hurt, or frustration don't magically go away. Still harbouring anger or resentment, expelled students may explode in other ways, committing crimes such as vandalism against the school or attacks on school staff. Admittedly, educators have a difficult job with complex problems. But displacement is not a good answer to discipline problems. Even when a student is "successfully" removed, the conflicts are only transferred from the school into society at large.

Have you ever seen two children fighting? Commonly, adults separate the two and ask them to make up. Sure enough, the children go through the motions of shaking hands. But the conflict is not resolved. Usually, one of two things happens. The children finish it themselves later, or there is a cold war. In contrast, two children who work it out to completion without adult intervention can often resolve their differences and become excellent friends.

Displacement is best thought of as a temporary measure that makes most sense when there are other emergencies that must be dealt with without delay; you wish to control the time and place of a confrontation; you are afraid the situation, if faced, might get dangerously out of hand (of course, as your conflict skill grows, your fear of these situations will lower accordingly); the long-term relationship with the conflicting party is unimportant; it is advisable, for safety reasons, to humour a deranged person; or nothing else has worked.

Displacement can provide the time to restore needed balance. Customer service representatives I've worked with report they sometimes butt heads with an angry customer. Nothing they do seems to work; the customer won't calm down or be appeased. Finally, in frustration, the customer service representatives refer the difficult customer to their supervisor, usually with a warning ("I've got a real difficult one this time"). The supervisor picks up the phone and, wonder of wonders, the customer is extremely polite. What happened?

Granted, the customer was difficult to start with, but the real problem probably developed when he and the customer service rep pushed on each other. Each was unwilling to yield; perhaps neither wanted to be a pushover or each feared losing face. Both became off-balance and rigid by emotionally bracing against the other. Passing this customer on to the supervisor provides a cooling-off period during which the customer can regain his balance. Often people in this situation are ashamed of their previously unreasonable stance or grateful for the end of the battle. So they go out of their way to be understanding, even to the point of apologizing to the supervisor!

You can use a cooling-off period anytime you and your "opponent" are at an impasse, or when you are afraid that either of you is losing control and will say or do something rash. If this happens in person, look him square in the eye, say you'll be right back, but you were just on your way to the bathroom. What can he say? Go to the bathroom and assume control of yourself. Use any technique that works quickly for you. Then you will be able to return on a better note to solve the problem.

Briefly displacing conflict during a phone call can also work well. Telephone communication has inherent limitations. There are fewer non-verbal cues to read, so body language communication doesn't work. Because of this, it is more difficult to make and maintain good contact with the caller, and therefore harder to resolve conflicts.

But the martial arts approach is to focus on the favourable aspects of any situation you're in. The advantage of phone calls is that you are invisible. If you are head-to-head with someone on the phone, consider a telephone time out. You can do this several ways.

- Ask if you can put them on hold so you can call up further information on your computer. Use the time to regain self-control. For these purposes, it doesn't really matter whether you have a computer or not.

- Tell them you must get further information from someone else and that you will call back within ten minutes.

- Hang up *on yourself*, then call them right back and apologize. This will often break a communication logjam. (This isn't a good strategy if you work for a telephone company.)

Remember, the point of a telephone time out, or of any cooling-off period, is to use the separation to regain your balance and composure. Unfortunately, we hear of labour dispute cooling-off periods that turn out to be anything but that. During these periods of separation, conflict instead builds as parties mentally replay discussions and incite themselves. Don't waste your time pumping up your anxiety; instead, lower your own energy level. Then you can make contact again with more control.

Displacement is often misused. Dealing with conflict can be uncomfortable, but avoiding or fleeing from conflict creates situations that, in the long run, are even more uncomfortable or dangerous. Remember that when you avoid conflict, the problem is not solved, only moved out of sight and hearing. That's well and good if you decide not to deal with that dissatisfied subordinate now. But if you want their loyalty and best efforts in the long term, be sure to schedule a time reasonably soon when you can resolve the problem. Putting people off indefinitely only generates lasting ill will.

Displacement can backfire if you use it with a highly charged person. For example, a very irritated customer will become even more upset if you put her off or pass her along. Have you ever called a business with a complaint, only to get transferred around? Most people become even more perturbed by this and their energy level will rise; if past the edge of their conflict curve they may hang up angrily or verbally explode at a hapless operator. The ones that don't release may harbour ill will toward that business for a long time. Remember this, if you do find it necessary to pass an angry person to another staff member: first help lower her energy level by listening—don't transfer her while she is seething, reassure her that you are taking personal responsibility for helping her ("I will make sure this gets straightened out"), stay in contact for a short time after you make the transfer (phone or in person) until you are sure she feels she is getting adequate assistance, offer your name and number as a backup, and follow up with her at a later date ("I wanted to make sure everything got resolved"). You can modify this approach to be effective with both subordinates and with external customers.

CREATIVE CONFLICT

Any strategy works in some situations; none works in all. A strong conflict manager is able to handle almost any kind of conflict—with short-fusers, slow-burners, or intimidators, whether the conflict is just beginning or almost peaked. Yet people tend to be more comfortable with one strategy than others. In the martial arts context of honest thinking, it's important to know what is your most preferred approach—fuelling/confrontation or avoidance/displacement?

Go beyond your self-set limits; don't trap yourself into one style. Where it's relatively safe, try other approaches. It's dangerous to attempt a new approach in a dangerous situation. The best way to learn something new is under low-stress conditions. The martial artist learns a new defence under controlled rules in practise sessions with a trusted partner, not in a life-and-death position. With this in mind, develop strength in defusing by selecting conflicts that are relatively safe—with close friends or less intimidating peers. Practising this way allows you to refine the technique, to develop your own modifications, and to increase your confidence.

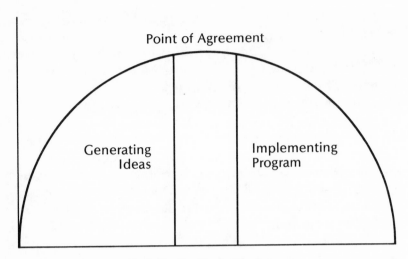

Figure 7. Conflict in Creativity

As previously indicated, expert martial artists create techniques they haven't previously seen; creativity emerges from their conflict. In the same way, conflict in dynamic organizations drives creativity. In the energy-building phase, ideas are generated. People disagree, perhaps strongly, but without their egos being lastingly threatened.

Momentum builds; this peaks at the point of agreement. Things reach a fever pitch as people ask, "What are we going to do? How?" Finally consensus emerges, as discussion turns into a plan of action. When talk and planning evolve into action, it can be a tense time of eliciting commitment and choosing direction. Tension lowers after agreement, and the energy is channelled into the real work.

Creative, dynamic organizations do see ups and downs, tension and conflict. Where there are people, there will be disagreements, insecurities, and different approaches. But their black-belt managers focus on converting this energy toward a positive end, to strengthen the organization and the people who are part of it.

DEFENDING AGAINST ROLE ATTACKS AND PERSONAL ATTACKS

It's not unusual for martial artists to be challenged by people wanting to test their fighting skills. One martial arts instructor was having a drink with an advanced student after class in a tavern. His equipment bag was partially open, revealing his black belt. A stranger approached the instructor and asked in a belligerent and slurred voice, "Are you a black belt?" "Yes," the *sensei* reluctantly answered; he watched the questioner. Within a few minutes the stranger screamed and rushed the instructor, who simply swivelled on the stool out of the line of attack. The man ran into the bar counter and knocked himself unconscious. The instructor caught him and gently lowered him to the ground. "Let's get out of here," he said to his student. And they left.

There was no real conflict between the instructor and the attacker—it takes two or more parties to make a conflict. It was merely a test of "a martial arts black belt," an example of a role attack. It wasn't a personal attack. The martial artist and managers should distinguish between these two basic forms. Differentiating between the two will enable you to respond more effectively to both.

Role attacks focus solely on a person's role. While individual employees react differently to their manager—some are approval-seeking, some are supportive, and others rebellious—this is generally not a personal response to the manager. (Of course, personal factors do enter into these relationships.)

A subordinate may confront a manager by saying, "What is the matter with you people in management? None of you know what is going on; no one does any planning! You messed up my vacation schedule again and I'm not going to stand for it!" This is not a *personal* attack, so don't take it as such. The "you people" and "none of you" categorize the manager as part of the *management of that company*.

Basically, in role conflict, one party attacks another on the basis of a class, or a stereotype. This can be directed to

- sex ("You're just like the other women executives.")

- job role ("You've done it again. Shot from the hip. That's a typical Marketing move.")

- job level (management vs. line staff, mid-management vs. upper-management)

- job category (white collar vs. blue collar or office staff vs. field personnel)

- location ("You people in the head office never understand our needs. You're up in the clouds.")

- race, religion, or national origin

- age ("Things are different now. What's the matter with your generation? Why can't you change with the times?")

- many others ("You single parents spend more time on the phone than
doing the job. That's why I can't get through when I need assistance."
"That's a typical response for your organization!" "You bureaucrats are
preventing me from getting my work done on time.")

Role attacks are worth hearing; they can show up interdepartmental
frustrations and anti-organizational attitudes that may need changing.
Listen for the message, but don't view them as personally threatening.

In contrast, personal attacks clearly stand out as direct, negative shots
at an individual. ("You've had it in for me ever since I was transferred
here. What's your problem?") But even when an attack is meant to be
personal, you don't have to respond to it as such. It's up to you whether
you do. Remember, even when you're under attack, there is no conflict
without your resistance. You can be in control.

The Technique of Untargetting

One of the first self-defence movements budding martial artists learn
is to *Get Off The Line.* That is, they move out of the path of the attack by
ducking, side-stepping, swerving, or doing anything that works. The
fancy kicks, punches, and throws can wait, because if a good blow
lands on you, you may not get another opportunity to launch your own
techniques.

Likewise, when 'a verbal, emotional attack is unleashed at you and
you don't wish to get hit, move out of the line of fire. To control a role
attack, don't respond in your role! When you hear "What is the matter
with you people in management?" don't say, "How dare you speak to
me that way? I'm your boss and don't you ever forget it. Do you want
to continue working here?" This kind of retaliation accelerates the
conflict; neither of you may be able to disengage before serious consequences occur.

Instead, respond *personally.* "Joe, I know how you feel. I'd get pretty
upset too if my vacation seemed up in the air. Give me some more
details. Let's see if we can straighten this out. By the way, where are
you planning to go?" A response to a role attack ("What the hell do you
managers know about sales anyway?") might be "Sharon, I'm sorry

about this problem" or "Not much beyond my summer selling job in college, Sharon. But I've been assigned to see this one through."

Notice the use of the first name. Actually, because non-verbal communication carries the meat of the message, the words are less important than the delivery in this situation. The key is to make your tone of voice informal; this is what makes a response personal. (It may not be appropriate in certain situations to call someone by first name.)

Similarly, when you're on the receiving end of a personal attack, respond in your role. To "You self-important s.o.b. You've had it in for me since I got here," you might reply, "Mr. Erickson, I am sorry that you are unhappy. You understand there are certain procedures we must follow. But, of course, we will do our best to work through your concerns. Now what is the specific problem?" Notice the use of the more formal address; more importantly, the tone is more distant, more in *role*.

Basically, this untargetting technique means not pushing back when a conflict is offered. It's easy to write about, but hard to do because it takes discipline. Most people's first response is to respond in kind. But a personal response to a personal attack actually enlarges the target; it's as if an arrow were flying your way and instead of ducking you puffed up and said, "OK, hit me!"

As a response, untargetting can disarm the strongest attack. Answer in a totally unexpected manner and use the power of distraction. The attacker is focused in front, on your role, but you come back from the side, as an individual.

Another disarming technique is distraction. Robert Button, a friend of mine and a holder of black belts in two martial arts, used distraction to avoid a fight. He was to meet his wife for dinner. Having arrived a few minutes early, he sat in the waiting area of the restaurant. An attractive woman smiled briefly at him. Just then, her boyfriend emerged from the restroom and became enraged. He raised his voice, shouting, "Trying to make time with my girl friend?" His energy level rose. But Robert took control by breaking in. "That's it! You remind me of my father! You sound just like he did when I came home from that camp." The would-be attacker was disarmed. Confused, he nodded, rejoined his girlfriend, and occasionally threw perplexed gazes at my friend.

It's not always easy to determine whether an attack is role-directed or personally directed, particularly where there is minimal communication. For example, an employee may seem disgruntled, yet be unwilling to discuss his problem. Or a supervisor may only receive negative feedback second-hand. But when you can tell whether an attack is mostly role or personal, use untargetting. Note that this strategy, like most conflict management techniques, does not solve the underlying problem. But it helps lower the conflict curve, prevents escalation, and puts you and the attacker in position to calmly problem-solve together and strengthen your working relationship.

NON-VERBAL TECHNIQUES FOR CONTROLLING CONFLICT

There are many techniques for controlling conflict. In all cases, however, bear in mind that the focus must be on controlling yourself, not others. Remember, "The greatest warrior conquers himself first." If you attempt to use the following techniques to control another, they will be far less effective and can even backfire. Your intention is crucial; others can read it. Also, these techniques are individual. What works for one person (or against one adversary) may not for another. Things are never the same. A method that defuses conflict between Joanne and Peter today may not work tomorrow during another conflict between the same two people.

These methods are predominantly non-verbal. There are 12 main factors in any conflict situation. Control them and you can direct the conflict.

Mental Techniques

1. Attitude. Martial artists work continuously on their attitude. What is your conflict attitude? Do you have a "victim" attitude? ("Oh no, I'm in for it now!") Or do you have a "punishing" attitude? ("How dare you challenge me. You'll pay for this!") Do you see conflict as destructive, as something that should always be smoothed over?

Some of the attitude control methods in the first section can help you develop a strong conflict-utilization attitude. You can learn to see that conflict is natural and healthy, and that you can direct it to desired goals.

2. Timing. Can you sense when others are receptive? How well do you stay in contact during conversation? Do you typically jump ahead

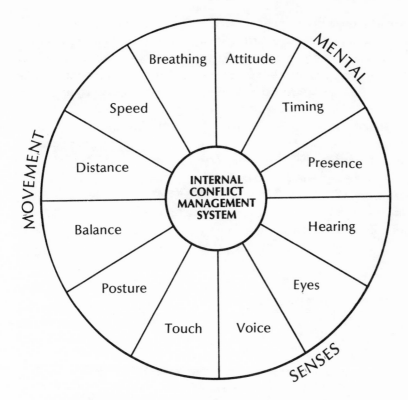

Figure 8. Non-verbal Techniques for Controlling Conflict

or lag behind others? Good timing involves seeing and using openings, and waiting for the space before intervening. Waiting is an art in itself. Discipline yourself to wait like a relaxed, yet fully alert cat by a gopher hole, ready to act when the opportunity presents itself.

Martial arts expert Walter Muryasz says people typically stay in contact with others for but a few moments when carrying on a social conversation, discussing a business deal, or executing a self-defence movement. They are impatient to get their point across and their job done. But openings usually appear and close quickly. By the time they are noticed and action is attempted, the opening has disappeared. So the moment of receptivity is gone, the opportunity has evaporated, and the person is on guard once more.

In contrast, good timing, Muryasz emphasizes, entails staying in close contact with the other person: "hugging the surface." If you're searching for a door opening in the dark, run your hands along the door surface, rather than patting for it. When a gap opens, you won't have to search for it, because you'll slip into it.

3. Presence. Have you ever met a martial arts master? They seem to be big, larger than their actual physical size. They have a strong presence—there's a feeling of great energy about them.

Presence comes from single-mindedness. It's the ability to be "present" with others. To increase your presence, practise focusing single-mindedly when you listen or speak with others. Discipline yourself not to become distracted by what has just occurred ("What did she mean by that?"), by what is going to happen ("Where is he going? Is he going to ask me to resign?"), or by thoughts about other places ("I wish I were in my garden right now"). If your mind races or dwells during conflicts, bring it back to the present so you don't miss anything important.

Techniques of the Senses

Ninja warriors were known for their ability to move easily in the dark and seem invisible to others. Attune yourself to ninja level by using the following techniques of the senses during conflict.

4. Hearing. How well do you listen? Can you hear without over-reacting to loaded words? ("You called me a what? How dare you!")

Use the copper wire technique. Copper is an excellent conductor that allows electricity to pass through it without being harmed itself. In contrast, a resistor is something that actively blocks the flow of electricity; it gets hot when current is passed through it. So when emotional current is coming your way, don't resist. If you do, you, too, will get hot.

Make sure both feet are flat on the ground. Imagine there is a copper wire running through the middle of your body from your head, down your torso, and splitting off into two branches through your legs, your feet, and into the ground. Allow the opponent's emotional current to pass through you, and be grounded out. Don't resist it and let it heat you up.

Listen fully to what the other person says. Allow your own reactions—emotions, thoughts, or physical feelings—to pass through the copper wire into the ground. Managers have reported this technique is especially easy to use over the phone where they can close their eyes to visualize the copper wire. This technique will help you to remain calm and be more perceptive.

Remain in control like a martial expert in a tense situation. Don't let yourself be goaded into a fight that does not serve you. To prevent your over-reacting to loaded words during a heated conversation, control your attention like a stereo: tune up the music, tune down the words. You won't miss anything important when you downplay the words and tune up an opponent's tone of voice and body language. You'll hear everything, but the words will be in the background. Since you're now less likely to take offence, it will be easier to help your opponent lower his energy level. Then, firmly in control, you can move on to productive problem-solving.

5. Eyes. Many martial arts instructors advise students to fight with "soft eyes." They teach how not to become focused on one thing, one part of the body, or person that you miss seeing other dangers. Open your vision. Focus "softly" and let your peripheral vision widen.

Managers can do the same thing during conflict. Practice widening and narrowing your attention span. Consciously shift your focus so you see both facial and body cues, even taking in onlookers' reactions, when these may be important. Use "soft eyes" and see the entire scene.

Don't get trapped into only seeing an opponent's eyes. A staring contest, or staredown, is a push-push conflict. Neither side wants to look away; this would be an admission of weakness or defeat. But sustaining this kind of eye conflict can be uncomfortable, or even escalate the discord. Try this simple martial arts technique as an alternative to giving in or playing "stare wars."

When the stare-off becomes uncomfortable, slightly shift your focus to a point between your opponent's eyes; now look at him with soft eyes, seeing his entire facial expression. This movement is so small that he won't be able to tell you're not looking him squarely in the eyes. But despite its subtlety, such a slight shift will relieve the tension and prevent your feeling overpowered. You'll both have an opportunity to back off and regain your mental balance.

6. Voice. Martial artists use their voices extensively. There is even one martial art, *kiaijitsu*, that focuses on sophisticated methods of shouting as its main weapon. Experts are said to be able to kill or paralyse opponents with just their voice as a weapon.

Such remarkable voice power is beyond the untrained person, but a trained, well-timed voice can strike fear into an opponent, distract

him, or focus one's own strength. For example, hypnotists use a sooth-
ing voice to instil calmness. Big animal trainers also use their voices to
take control and forestall attacks.

Practice modulating your voice. Basically, the voice is a wind instru-
ment whose sound comes from breathing through the larynx and a
formed mouth. Breathing exercises can aid voice control until you
develop the ability to raise or lower vocal pitch and volume at will.

People who tend to displace, that is, to avoid or suppress conflict,
often have voices that operate mostly on the soft side. If you are like
this, I suggest you practise turning up your vocal volume at times.

Those who are prone to fuelling conflict by accelerating or confronting the situation, may wish to work on lowering and slowing their
voice when they become angry. Anytime you are alone and out of
earshot, you can practise changing voice pitch, speed, and volume.
Driving alone with the car windows rolled up is one good time to
practice.

7. Touch. Except for the expert in kiaijitsu (see above), martial
artists work through touch. Especially in the throwing arts, all of
which control another's balance, it's vital to develop a sensitive and
strong touch. And at the work place, touching can either escalate threat
or help defuse a conflict, depending on the circumstances. How comfortable are you with touch? Do you know when it is appropriate to
touch someone else?

If touch is to be an effective means of dealing with a conflict, it helps
to know how to read another's "touchability." The research of Dr. John
Kappas (in his *Professional Hypnotism Manual*) is interesting. *Generally*,
he says, you can tell in advance whether someone is comfortable being
touched. People who accept touching tend to touch other people themselves and to use broad gestures when they talk. They also tend to wear
loose-fitting clothing. On the other hand, those who don't like being
touched tend to speak with limited hand gestures, not touch others,
and wear more tailored clothing. Making physical contact with a "no-
touch" person can escalate a conflict. In contrast, a calm, relaxed touch
on those who are comfortable with it can calm emerging antagonism.

Know where to touch. This depends on who the other person is
and his or her cultural orientation—a spouse, best friend, casual co-
worker, or first-time customer. It's best not to use touching to defuse
conflict if it might be interpreted as a sexual advance.

Generally, it's also wise to avoid touching a co-worker's face, head, arms, or back of hands. This can be seen as patronizing or overly intimate. In Western culture, the shoulders are usually the safest place to touch. If you're operating in a different culture, learn how touching might be interpreted there.

Know how to touch. It's better not to approach a person quickly or directly from the front. This may seem as if you're rushing the person and can induce a protective reaction. It's preferable to move closer slowly and from the side. In addition, pushing down too hard on someone conveys that you're trying to dominate. At the other extreme, touching too softly may communicate weakness or unsureness.

Touch is a useful conflict-defusing technique only when both you and the other person are comfortable with it. You don't necessarily have to know in advance whether this will work. Just pay attention. If you begin to touch someone, and he starts to tense, back off. If you still insist on touching, he'll see it as an attack.

Movement Techniques

Moving like a martial artist can keep you in control and safer during conflict.

8. Posture. In chapter three, we examined the ways posture can affect your emotional state. Your posture also influences others' perceptions of you during conflict.

I have shown photos of people in various postures to thousands of managers. Amazingly, they report similar results: People who are slumped (C-shaped posture) are seen as weak, disinterested, unapproachable, or bored. People who assume a rigid, I-shaped posture are described as aggressive, tense, or rigid. When someone maintains a natural, S-shaped posture, he is seen as relaxed, confident, equal, and approachable.

By consciously assuming the appropriate posture, you can enhance communication and your control of conflict. And don't slip into a posture that contradicts what you are trying to do. Saying "OK, I'll give in and do it your way" while assuming an I-shaped posture is not effective because it sends out a mixed message. This will either confuse the other person or lower your credibility. Others tend to believe your non-verbal communication and disregard your words, so it is best to have them in agreement.

In the right situation each posture has advantages. For example, use a C-shaped posture when

- Someone is intimidated by you and you want to offset your threatening appearance. Slumping will make you appear weaker.

- You want to emphasize that you are giving in to another's demands. This can be an excellent way to placate someone's anger.

Assume an I-shaped posture when

- You wish to show you are unyielding on this point, that "the line is drawn here."

- You're attempting to overpower someone.

And a natural S-shaped posture is best when

- You wish to communicate on an equal level.

- You want to feel—and be—relaxed and confident.

9. Balance. Martial artists know that the more balanced they are, the stronger and more relaxed they'll be. Black belts have long known that your state of balance communicates your vulnerability to others.

Communications professor Betty Grayson wanted to determine whether non-verbal communication affected "attackability." She showed ten-second silent videotapes of different people walking to a prison audience of convicted murderers, muggers, and rapists. The audience rated each person's "assault potential," on a scale of one ("most assaultable, a very easy rip-off") to ten ("would avoid them, too big a situation, too heavy"). The filmed subjects were males and females of all ages.

After the criminals had rated the victims, she took the clips of the most attackable people (rated one through three) and the least attackable (rated eight through ten) to someone trained in Labanalysis, a form of body movement notation. Professor Grayson asked this expert whether there were any differences between the two groups and whether the members of each group had anything in common.

The Labanalyst said that the most and least attackable people showed markedly different body movements. According to an article in the *Washington Post*, Grayson reported that "five movement characteristics were common to all the selected victims. First was the way they lifted their feet. Instead of walking from heel to toe, they picked up their whole foot and put it down—like a Spanish dancer. They all used exaggerated strides, either too long or too short. And they moved laterally. Instead of swinging their right arm with their left leg, they moved the same arm as leg. Then there was the way the top of their body moved in conjunction with the bottom of their body. It was as though their torso moved at cross-purposes, with the right shoulder moving in conjunction with their left hip. And they walked so that their arm and leg movements appeared to come from outside their body instead of from within. Although women in the '45 and older' group were nearly twice as likely [as other people] to be judged easy victims, an equal number of men and women in the '35 and under' group were picked as easy targets."

I suspect "45 and older women" were deemed most attackable because of culture, not sex. Perhaps these women grew up during a period when it was less acceptable for females to appear physically robust.

Usually, when someone is intimidated, his balance drifts back over his heels, making him an emotional and physical "pushover." Control your balance. Enhance how strong you feel. Don't lean away or be off-balance during conflicts.

10. Distance. Positioning is critical in any conflict or competition. One way to control position is to choose the correct distance; this allows you to use leverage most effectively. In face-to-face communication, it's important to make good contact. Too great a physical distance in conflict dilutes emotional contact; too small a space can be threatening. Again, the appropriate non-verbal working distance between people is determined by relationships. In some cultures, it's considered rude and emotionally cold not to be able to smell the other's body odours; in others, more distance is considered proper. In relationships, we generally tolerate friends and family standing closer to us than strangers.

Some people are "space invaders." They attempt to intimidate by getting too close. But you don't have to allow yourself to be taken off-balance this way.

You can keep them at arms length. When they begin to move in, pat them on the shoulder. *Pat down, not away*. This will tend to plant them in place. If you push them *away*, you invite escalation.

When the Space Invader moves in, turn to the side. People will tolerate someone standing closer to them side-by-side than squarely in front. Turn your head and speak to them shoulder to shoulder. This will help you feel less attacked and more in control.

11. Speed. On the mat or in a fight, your speed is important. Move too slowly, and you can lose an advantage. But faster isn't always better. Sometimes, performing a martial arts technique too quickly can wake up an opponent. It's often better to wait until they are really off-balance before making your move.

Consciously control your speed. When the conflict is close to the top of its curve, rapid motion can trigger a strong defensive reaction. Practise slowing down and speeding up your intensity of motion and voice, at will. Besides helping you control conflict, being able to change your pace will also help command attention during presentations.

12. Breathing. Breathing indicates the state of excitement. So, learn to control your breathing. Don't hold your breath during conflict. Remember, you want your brain fully oxygenated and alert. Read others' breathing in order to perceive their level of anger.

By reading these non-verbal factors, you can recognize the rising and falling of conflict energy in yourself and in others. By controlling these factors in yourself, you can influence the course of the conflict.

In the martial arts, everything is interrelated. When and how you move influences your opponent's response, which, in turn, affects you. Communication is never linear. All of the above non-verbal factors are interrelated; changing any factor affects the others.

Controlling your breath immediately affects your voice. Slight changes in posture will correspondingly adjust your balance. And a small attitude shift can influence your ability to maintain eye contact. So it's not necessary to try to control all of these factors. This would take too much effort.

Moving the hub of the axle most efficiently moves a wheel; understanding this, martial artists seek to control the centre of a conflict. The centre of any conflict is your Internal Conflict Management System. Your relationship with yourself is its foundation. It is the centre from which conflict-handling ability ripples out.

Compare two days, one when you are feeling internally peaceful and another when you woke up on the wrong side of the bed. On both days, a car cuts you off and nearly causes an accident, or someone sneers at your favourite project. You react very differently on the two days. On your better days, you are not as easily upset.

Using the Techniques for Immediate and Long-Term Improvement

Note the two or three factors in conflict control that you presently feel comfortable with. These are part of your bag of tricks. You may now be able to sustain eye contact or you may have excellent timing. Also note your present limitations, those factors you currently have difficulty with or are uncomfortable using. In any given conflict, there's no way to predict what will work best. Try something—if one factor doesn't help, try another in which you feel proficient.

To make immediate changes in your ability to control conflict, focus on your strengths and steer clear of your weaknesses. If you know your voice cracks nervously during confrontations, defuse the conflict through your excellent listening skills. Immediate gains will come by using present techniques. Save experimentation for practice sessions or other low-threat situations.

To make long-range changes in your ability to control conflict, transform your limitations into strengths or, at the least, neutralize them as weaknessess. If you tend to jump into discussions too often, work on your timing. This approach takes longer than focusing on current strengths, but it is an excellent way of strengthening your conflict management range. Moreover, your overall self discipline will strengthen.

Use these methods at home as well as at work, with family and friends as well as with co-workers. Conflicts are common during these changing times. But you can harness them to strengthen yourself, others, and your organization.

The Martial Art of Conflict: Techniques for Action

- Observe how you become emotionally involved in conflict. Know your fears. Watch your reactions; don't try to stop your emotions, but do let them pass by like scenes in a motion picture. Remind yourself that anticipation creates fear. Does your voice become squeaky or scratchy when you're nervous? Is it artificially husky when you are trying to be assertive?

- Assess your usual style of dealing with conflict. In which situations is this style most and least effective? Experiment with different approaches.

- Change negative attitudes about conflict; think of using it as an ally. How has it already helped your organization and you? Whenever there is a conflict, think how you can channel the resulting energy toward organizational ends.

- Notice managerial controls. How thick is your policies and procedures manual? Delete rules that are unnecessary or create too much resistance.

- Monitor the conflict climate. How do staff in your organization escalate conflict by pushing back?

- Catch yourself in a blindly forceful mode.

- Watch how conflict builds over time. Which employees are slow-burners and which have short fuses?

- Practise your timing. Restrain your intervention until there is a receptive moment.

- Learn to recognize motorset in everyday activities.

- Observe a bully and objectively observe how he sets up intimidation.

- Consciously decide whether it's best to Fuel, Avoid, or Defuse each conflict. With time, these decisions will become more and more instinctive.

- Practise differentiating between personal and role attacks. Shift into your role when personally confronted and shift into a personal response when attacked in role.

- Remind yourself that you are not the target. When you are in the path of a car, handcart, or person coming your way, practise "stepping off the line." Apply this technique to verbal conflict situations.

- Observe where distraction and humour can momentarily divert a building conflict.

- What is your conflict management history? Honestly assess your own conflict attitudes and how they help and limit you.

- Practise looking for openings. There's no need to force them. When you calmly watch, they will jump out at you.

- Take account of your two or three non-verbal conflict strengths, as well as your two or three greatest weaknesses. Make more use of your present strengths. In less threatening situations, practise your weaker skills.

PART III

MASTERING CHANGE

Change is the order of heaven and earth . . . To remember troubled days in days of peace and to constantly train one's body and mind form guiding spirit and character.

Gichin Funakoshi, *Karate-do: My Way of Life*

Within constant motion and change there is tranquility, and within tranquility there is motion and change.

Prof. Henry Seishiro Okazaki, *The Esoteric Principles of Judo*

In nature, things move violently to their place and calmly in their place.

Sir Francis Bacon

CHAPTER SEVEN

Responding to Change

In this uncertain world, ours should be the path of discipline.

Shiba Yoshimasa, Chikubasho

> *Men knowing the Way of life*
> *Respect their foes,*
> *They face the simple fact before it becomes involved.*
> *Solve the small problem before it becomes big.*
> *The most involved fact in the world*
> *Could have been faced when it was simple,*
> *The biggest problem in the world*
> *Could have been solved when it was small.*
> *The simple fact that he finds no problem big*
> *Is a sane man's prime achievement.*
> *If you say yes too quickly*
> *You may have to say no,*
> *If you think things are done too easily*
> *You may find them hard to do:*
> *If you face trouble sanely*
> *It cannot trouble you.*

Lao Tzu, Tao Te Ching

SELF-DEFENCE AND CHANGE

Life never stands still; situations are never the same. In *The Tao of Jeet Kune Do*, Bruce Lee wrote, "The stillness in stillness is not the real stillness; only when there is stillness in movement does the universal rhythm manifest itself. To change with change is the changeless state." Changes can be like a sudden attack, springing in an instant, or like a slow wave, or a steadily marching army. However it approaches, change is inescapable. Stability only comes from being able to float safely on each wave of change.

When tae kwon do students begin their training, they kick the air hundreds, even thousands of times, for balance, flexibility, and body alignment. But kicking the air is easy and doesn't approximate real life. So the students spar to get practise in defending against constantly changing attacks. In a sense, the martial artist puts in years of training for an attack he hopes will never occur, developing the habit of being watchfully alert and ready for anything.

Nevertheless assaults may still occur. Late one night, after flying home from a business trip, I stopped to pick up mail at my postal box. As I turned the corner to the post office I saw two men laughing and cursing each other as they passed a bottle. Minding my own business, I walked around them. Just then, out of the corner of my eye, I saw one of them kick out at me. Without thinking, I sidestepped and moved in on him, with my hands up and ready. He fell back against the building wall. "Really sorry, just kidding," he stammered. No harm was done. They hadn't touched me nor I them, so I went about my business. All of this happened in the space of a few seconds, which was too fast to think.

Responding to change means both preparation for the sudden attack and awareness of the more gradual patterns of growth and decline. By charting things, watching how they grow, you can prevent disasters that might have been. Perceiving and avoiding small problems, paying attention even to the "trifles" (see chapter one), can avert the larger, life-threatening ones. As a manager, for example, when you are aware that growing worker dissatisfaction is building, you can act (document the dissatisfaction to prove to others the need for new policies, and adjust those practices contributing to low morale) to forestall a major problem.

Sun Tzu wrote, in the classic *The Art of War,* "It is functional military law that one does not rely on the enemy not coming, but relies on the fact that he himself is waiting; one does not rely on the enemy not attacking, but relies on the fact that he himself is unassailable."

In real life, when plans are made in a void, they are easily foiled by changing situations, countered by new ground rules, or frustrated by sudden changes in the financial market. Competitors rarely hold true to our initial assessments of them.

Why is managing change so difficult? Life often feels like a multiple attack; issues and problems never come as you expect. It's like driving on a multi-lane highway where other drivers don't follow the rules of the road. Their speed varies and many act unpredictably, even to the point of jeopardizing their, and your, life. The only way to protect yourself and get to where you want to go is to be ready for anything, just like the martial artist. Be prepared for swervings or stops in any direction. When these do occur, use free technique (*jiuwaza*); create a defence; don't wed yourself to set forms. Sounds both hazy and complex? This is why managing change is an advanced skill, challenging even high-ranking black belts.

Clearly, expert managers, like martial artists, have to be open and ready to adapt to anything that comes their way: your main product is involved in an unfortunate and much-publicized death; changing demographics reduce the demand for your most profitable services.

Shifting technology, regulations, markets, and staff reactions affect most organizations. The accelerating pace of work life can make it difficult to know how to react or make effective decisions. Especially during these swirling, competitive times, mastering change can make the difference between business strength and bare survival or worse. Because black-belt managers eschew seeing themselves as victims, they develop strategies for reacting to uncontrollable change. Self defence is easier when you can see the threat at an early stage. So they start by amplifying *aware* concentration.

There is a well-known Japanese folk tale about a great swordsmaster who demonstrated to a visitor the teaching he had given his three sons. He wedged a heavy vase on the corner of a sliding door so that it would fall on whomever entered the room. Then he called for his oldest son. Before opening the door, the son sensed the danger. He slid open the door, caught the falling vase, then entered and replaced it over the door. The swordsmaster introduced his son to the visitor, "This is my oldest. He has learned well. One day, he will master *kenjutsu* [swordsmanship]."

The father called for his second son, who entered without hesitating and only caught the vase just before it struck his head. "This is my middle son. He is improving, but still has much to learn." Then the youngest son was summoned. He entered hurriedly and was struck a heavy blow by the vase. But before it could hit the floor, a quick stroke of the boy's sword cut the vase in two. "This is my youngest. He still has a long way to go."

In times of change, narrow concentrations won't do. Most people are surrounded by concerns, challenges, and problems. There is rarely only one thing going on at a time. So if you brace hard against one problem and block others out, you risk being blindsided and over-whelmed. Rather, develop a 360-degree readiness, without anticipating an attack from any one direction.

An impatient young man asked a great swordsman to take him as a student. Seeing latent talent and clear desire, the martial artist agreed. He instructed the eager young man to start his learning by cleaning the house and stables. The young man worked at this admirably, but as days became months, he grew more frustrated. One day he approached the master. "Sir, you agreed to take me as a martial arts student. Yet all I have done so far these months is simple chores."

The swordsman assured the student that if he would continue with his duties, his practice would begin in earnest. From that day on, the student was never safe. During the young man's work, the master would suddenly leap out and beat him soundly with a *shinai* (bamboo sword). The student was determined to continue and over time learned to anticipate the master's attacks. While the attacks didn't abate, he was able to avoid an ever-greater percentage of beatings.

Many months later, the student happened upon the master making soup. "Now is my chance to get even," thought the young man. As the swordsman was stirring the pot with one hand and holding the lid with the other, the student soundlessly crept close, and suddenly aimed a ferocious blow at the master's head with a broom handle. Without interrupting his stirring, the swordsman calmly raised the lid and blocked the blow.

The moral of this famous martial arts tale is that you can concentrate fully on the task at hand without leaving yourself vulnerable to unexpected blows. In *The Tao of Jeet Kune Do,* Bruce Lee explained, "A concentrated mind is not an attentive mind, but a mind that is in the state of awareness can concentrate." Awareness is never exclusive; it includes everything. One way to practise this state of awareness is by strengthening your peripheral vision. When you are reading, let your senses expand to take in the desk and room. Be aware of this peripheral information in the background while you read. Simultaneously seeing both foreground and background will take practice, but you can develop this awareness (hint—use soft eyes, as explained in the previous chapter).

Do you remember the last time you were startled? Martial artists know that being startled is a sign of too narrow concentration. Have you ever noticed the reaction of someone after you turned a corner and unexpectedly came face-to-face with him? He freezes. When a person "jumps out of his skin," he's too tense and vulnerable because he's unable to react quickly to changing circumstances. You can control the startle reflex by reminding yourself to keep your shoulders down and relaxed. This body-leverage strategy will help you react quickly and with balance to unexpected events. You'll still experience a rush of feeling when you're surprised, but you will be able to react and move.

To respond successfully to change, black-belt managers are aware of the changes that affect daily work. These include growing financial uncertainty, shifting values and expectations, increased competition on all levels, litigation, rapid shifts in technology, a movement of personnel to the service sector, a new mix of people in the work place, different governmental regulations, and reductions in management levels. There are many social changes that also affect the work place. Volumes have been written about these and other factors.

"Change is always stressful," notes IBM medical consultant Dr. Alan McLean. "It always involves losing something." Even relatively minor changes can be uncomfortable; for example, the street on which you normally drive home is closed for repaving or your favourite TV show is moved to a new night. But there are many more important, uncontrollable changes. When your company merges with another, the market shifts strongly, or your new boss has a markedly different style from your old one—many people initially feel overwhelmed, helpless, out of control. Finding oneself in one of these situations is like being a martial artist who, while minding his own business, is attacked by several assailants. What can we do when we feel attacked from all sides?

STAYING CALM UNDER PRESSURE

Judo master Henry Seishiro Okazaki noted, "Only by cultivating a receptive state of mind, without preconceived ideas or thoughts, can one master the secret art of reacting spontaneously and naturally without hesitation and without purposeless resistance."

Controlling yourself is the key to reacting successfully to change. Once again, this is something that's easier to say than to do. Think of clicking yourself into a calm mode (practice will make you more facile at this). By being flexible, alert, and watchful, you will be more able to swim in an ocean of uncontrollable change. Calmness does not mean never being ruffled; it's natural for strong winds to agitate the sea. But the deeper the water, the calmer it is. Stay down within yourself; concentrate on relaxing your hara, your centre of gravity.

Find calmness within movement. In *The Zen Way To The Martial Arts,* Taisen Deshimaru wrote, "Tranquility in movement is the secret of *kendo,* the way of the sword." He further wrote, "Look at a top: at first, when it's spinning slowly, it wobbles, it moves; then, when it has gathered momentum, it becomes stable and no longer moves. And at the end, like an old man, it starts to totter again, and at last it topples over."

Pressuring yourself to hold still during times of great change is like "forcing" yourself to relax—it doesn't work. Use movement to help create your stability. Be a warrior, not a worrier: active outside, but calm within.

It's difficult to relax under pressure, but extremely helpful. Bruce Lee wrote, "Not being tense but ready, not thinking yet not dreaming, not being set but flexible—it is being wholly and quietly alive, aware and alert, ready for whatever may come." Visualize yourself being alert and relaxed. Don't allow fear to control you. Remember your strengths and remind yourself of other changes you have previously weathered. This is the time to practise some of the attitude control exercises in the first section.

Retain your equanimity. During a fracas, remind yourself that all things pass, and react in the best possible way. In *Wisdom From the Ninja Village of the Cold Moon,* Stephen Hayes explains, "The *ninja* gains his perspective by expanding his perceptions to see that everything is change and reality is at best temporary."

In your professional life you will surely face some uncomfortable situations. When the merger is announced, or you've received word your budget will be cut by thirty percent, stay calm inside yourself. Let discomfort reside on the surface. Be patient with yourself when learning new procedures. Once again you're a white belt; just focus on what you have to do to become a black belt.

Neal McKenzie is a manager and engineer with Northrop, an electronics firm. In his spare time, Neal is a black-belt martial arts instructor. He's used martial arts principles to remain resilient in dealing with constant changes in his professional field. Neal was trained at Stanford University in vacuum tube technology. Since then there have been at least two revolutions in the field—transistors and microchips. In many professions, Neal's gray hair would be a sign of respected experience. But not in the fast-changing world of electronic engineering, where graying signifies obsolescence. But Neal is respected by his staff because he has stayed current with the principles and practices of his profession and handles his workload very well.

BEFRIENDING CHANGE

Make change work for you. Say you're surrounded by many attackers or threatening changes; with the right attitude and correct movement, you can actually turn multiple attackers to your advantage. Move in the right way and they'll get in each other's way, making it harder to reach you. Maybe you can use one as a shield against the others. Or confuse them and dictate the timing of the defence.

The Chinese symbol for great change is composed of two characters, one meaning "danger" and the other "opportunity." Any change really has both positive and negative elements. Happenings that appear to be the most dire always contain positive elements. In every recession, for example, many people lose money, but there are always some who do very well by focusing on the opportunities created.

Anytime an evidently negative change comes, look for the hidden benefits. Budget cuts mean a chance to manage more creatively, to use more leverage (finding ways to do more with less), or to learn new skills. One manufacturing division manager, seeing the writing on the organizational wall, accepted early retirement to pursue an old dream of taking an equity position in a high-tech environment. A colleague went into business for himself. Neither manager wasted energy bemoaning the changes that came; they rode the currents toward an advantageous position.

On the other side, remember there will always be negative outcomes from seemingly idyllic changes. Winning the lottery may strike you as totally wonderful, but there will be more taxes to pay, financial decisions to make, a loss of privacy, and a deluge of new "friends." If you balance your perspective, you will be able to embrace the opportunities that lie in seemingly negative changes and avoid potential dangers in windfalls.

Some change is just part of a wider landscape. "There has been a lot of organizational change at Shearson," says Karen Nish, "but that's appropriate; there's been a lot of change in the [stock] market."

Most of all, remember that you're not helpless. There are many things you can do in advance to prepare yourself for periods of great change. Put support systems in place when things are going smoothly; this way they'll be ready when the gale hits. Support systems that can especially help during changing times include your personal philosophy/mission statement, a strong guide when change threatens to unhinge you. Family relationship can help anchor you while you ride out changes at work that threaten to capsize you. Contrastingly, work can provide an anchor for short-term relationship storms.

Cultivate the supportive relationships of trusted colleagues and friends. Regularly have lunch or coffee with peers, and seek them out during times of difficult change. Discuss both your frustrations and plans for action with them. They can offer many kinds of support. First, you can go to a friend, close the door, and let your hair down, knowing what you say will not be repeated. Second, your confidant can suggest strategy options you may not see, simply because stress creates tunnel vision; you may miss what is clear to others. The third kind of support—the rarest and most valuable—comes when another person, upon hearing your repeated complaints, kicks you into action. ("I've heard you sing this song many times. You sound like a broken record. When are you going to get up and do something about it?")

Also, there are professional associations. Attend the meetings no matter what your position or field. Others who have gone through similar circumstances can provide perspective and model solutions to your problems.

Your favourite leisure or recreational activities can help. Even this takes discipline! Under duress, the last thing you may think of is leisure. But recreation can provide you the perspective and stress release you need to make strong, long-term decisions.

CONTROLLING YOUR POSITION: BE WATER, NOT ROCK; BE ROCK, NOT WATER

The martial artist knows that in self defence, there is a time to penetrate and time to yield. Two useful sayings are "Be rock, not water" and "Be water, not rock." When things are in an uproar around you and your staff is stressed and consumed with fear, "Be rock, not water." Stand firm and hold your position. Be a pillar of stability; reaffirm that everything will work out. In the midst of one major departmental change, the staff found itself well below its work quota; predictably, they began to blame the change plan. The manager became a rock. Holding firm, he reminded them that the plan had worked until then, that it was good and would work again. Their confidence came back as the wave of fear passed. He then helped them figure out how to restore lost productivity to its expected level.

But when confronted with resistance to change, when fear turns staff or customers into stone, "Be water, not rock." In *The Diary of the Way,* Andrew Lum is quoted as saying, "With flexibility you can change to any position. Like water, we must be able to change to all forms. If a room is filled with water and there is a small hole in the floor, one inch by one inch, all the water will escape. But suppose there is a rock two inches by one inch. It cannot escape; it is trapped. If you are like water you can escape through even the smallest of openings."

You don't have to allow resistance to stop you; you can flow around it. Is it difficult to calm employees' fear of layoffs from pending automation? Flow around the fear. Acknowledge their resistance and go ahead with your plans. Don't let unfounded fears block the new system.

There are times to become Rock, situations to become Water. The black belt art is in knowing which approach to choose.

BE READY AND ABLE TO MOVE

The Chinese masters taught students never to distribute their weight equally between the feet because when so "double-weighted," they could not move quickly in the event of a sudden attack. Any good *karate-ka* knows that attempting to kick with the weight still on his striking leg will cost him his balance. He must first transfer his weight to his supporting foot.

"In general, the body weight should not be divided fifty percent on each foot," tai chi ch'uan master Andrew Lum writes in *Diary of the Way.* "When the weight is divided unevenly you are most flexible. There is one free foot with which to move in any direction."

Too much stability makes it difficult to move, and bracing is dangerous. Of course, taken to the other extreme, putting all the weight on one foot deprives you of some balance. The masters recommend having an 80/20 distribution of weight. During times of change, if you are leaning the wrong way, you will be highly vulnerable. Look for and leave yourself room to move to a new position.

Similarly, black-belt managers don't double-weight. They value being ready to move and don't spread their operating base too wide. They aren't overly committed to stability. They maintain contact with the minority points of view. This helps them stay ready to shift their stance when the situation warrants.

The same applies in a broader sense to organizations. For example, developing too much manufacturing capacity can be dangerous; this may prevent you from being willing or able to adapt to changing consumer desires.

This is one of the reasons it's a wise idea to keep policies lean and few. Too many make you heavy and unable to move quickly. To transfer weight (shift your direction), you'll have to make intermediate moves and reassess all policies before you recast them. Only then will you be able to move. So keep focused on mobility; don't anchor your organization to policies that focus on what *not* to do.

Control your sphere of influence. Remind yourself to focus on what you can control (yourself), and directly influence (your own organizational unit). If you overextend yourself and try to do everything you see needed in the corporation, you'll only lose your balance. Do your own job and help those you directly work with to do theirs.

Many managers report feeling overwhelmed and unable to keep up with changes in their field; there is so much data available these days. By sharpening yourself into an efficient information processor, you will be able better to anticipate and to react to industry-wide changes. Listen and read carefully to sift out the vital nuggets of information you need. Decide which sources of information to scan and which you may put aside without loss. Make productive use of your time by using high-leverage technology that lightens your load—microcomputers, microcassette recorders when travelling, or mobile phones.

When changes come—as they will—you will be prepared. Rather than fight them, you will direct their movement to your benefit. By searching for opportunities, you will be positioned to make an ally of any change that threatens, and you will be calm and victorious.

Reacting to Change: Techniques for Action

- Remind yourself that everything changes and nothing is static. There is really no such thing as maintaining market share; you must re-win it each quarter.

- Use your self discipline especially when adverse changes strike. Don't let yourself bow to desperation. Do what is necessary to make yourself unassailable.

- Assess the broad changes affecting your organization. Don't miss the subtle ones. Cast your information nets wide so you see the change when it is still in the offing.

- Make a habit of keeping your shoulders down. Notice your reactions when you do become surprised.

- Practise mental readiness in your favourite sport or when driving. Relax and watch. Don't allow others' unexpected moves to throw you.

- Work on concentrating with awareness while reading, doing paper-work, or talking with someone. A good time to enlist this skill is during a group presentation, when you're answering an individual's question. Focus on the questioner, but be able to see peripherally the entire group's reaction.

- When you get beaten, learn from it. Don't make the same mistakes over and over again; at least, make different ones.

- Remember to manage the stress in any change.

- Practise the art of waiting without tension, like a cat at a mouse hole.

- Assess when to "Be rock, not water," and to hold your position; when to "Be water, not rock," and to flow around fear or resistance.

- Remember it's possible to be comfortable with being uncomfortable.

- Look for advantages even during the most dangerous periods of change.

- Develop supports you can harness in the face of change.

- Be ready and able to move quickly, don't be double-weighted. Watch out for areas where you are braced or too emotionally invested.

CHAPTER EIGHT

The Martial Art of Strategy: Planning to Achieve Change

The strategist makes small things into big things.

Miyamoto Musashi, *The Book of Five Rings*

If one plans to abide in a place for one year, he should plant the five grains. If his plan is for ten years, he should plant trees. If one's plans are for his whole life, there is nothing like sustaining his retainers.

Sixteenth-century Japanese proverb

Only by moving with focus can one have stability. Only by being stable can one have peace. Only by having peace can one be secure. Only in security can one deliberate. And only with deliberation will one be able to obtain.

Anonymous

   Ultimately, the martial artist's most powerful weapon is his mind. This "secret" weapon is the source of strategy: the ability to plan for, see, and make use of opportunities. Whoever masters the skills of strategy has the power to survive and act effectively, in both adverse and bountiful times.
   In both the martial arts and management, strategy is the art of making choices that move you towards goals and strengthen your position, without leaving you overly vulnerable. Each martial arts style is a strategy designed to protect the practitioner in specific situations by making the most of his position. For example, several *kung fu* styles mimic animal movements; the "white crane style," with its broad "wing" blocks, is excellent for long-range fighting; and the famous "drunken style" is designed to lull an opponent into believing his

intended victim is drunk and unable to defend himself; that is, until a surprise flurry of apparently haphazard moves defeats the attacker. Some martial arts focus on what to do when you are attacked in a kneeling or lying position.

Any management style is a strategy appropriate for certain situations and less appropriate in others. And every option has its price. The martial artist learns that the more stable a stance he assumes (lying down, for example), the less mobile he will be. Generally, the price of a greater ability to move is a reduction in balance. The wise strategist keeps in mind that situations change; a previously strong approach may become weak under different circumstances. When you deliver power—punch, kick, push—it is best to be solidly planted; when you receive power—get kicked or punched—it makes sense to be loosely connected with the ground so as to absorb the force by "floating away."

To become both fluid and well-balanced, the martial artist looks for and uses counterbalancing forces. You may have seen a karate expert throwing a forward punch with his right hand, while simultaneously drawing back his left. This combined movement both provides him with a powerful thrust and prevents his becoming overextended and off-balance.

Organizationally, a plan that retains a large degree of freedom of movement may leave you less stable and more vulnerable. A wise strategist sees the potential negative outcomes in any proposed change and plans to minimize them. He balances the costs of a change against its returns; for example, the effort required to institute new procedures against the time to be recouped when the new ways eventually take hold. Most planners consider these factors, but, in my experience, too many inaccurately assess the underlying cost of any change: reduced trust and increased suspicion, possible resistance, and lower productivity. If you don't consider staff resistance to change, you will have no plan to minimize it.

Two critical strategic elements in the martial arts are timing and position. In *Strategy In Unarmed Combat,* Paul Maslak writes of the martial arts strategist, "Even before the first kick is blocked, he has planned how to use his physical advantages most effectively against the opponent's disadvantages." That is, he has planned the process of action, reaction, and further action.

In combat, the ideal position protects you, allows you to use your force most efficiently, and lets you react easily when things change. In reality, the ideal position changes from moment to moment, as conditions shift. Clouds pass over the sun, the lay of the land changes, or the opponent varies his attitude and line of attack.

In managing, your decision about the ideal position to take will also be determined by market and financial conditions, competitors' approach, employee morale, and other factors. Just as martial artists search for an edge, creative managers try to spot potential for positive change, even when everyone else believes the situation is fixed. Larry Vance, an owner-manager of a small restaurant chain, has found his edge in training. Most of his competitors believe staff training is wasted on employees in a high turnover industry. But Larry realizes the way he treats staff will be passed on to customers as better quality service, so he aims to make work inspiring and enjoyable. By providing his employees with strong training in line with a clear mission, he reaps the benefits of return customers and lowered turnover costs.

Your position will determine how and what you see. The closer you stand to something, the more detail you will see in it. This is probably why the grass seems greener in the neighbour's yard; i.e., other organizations have fewer problems than we do. From afar, it is difficult to see all but broad patterns—divots, weeds, and other flaws are more easily perceived only as you get closer to the field.

So, when you wish to assess specific problems of performance or morale, get closer to the field. Don't hole up in your office and allow yourself to be surprised. Move out and see the lay of the land. Spend time with staff from different levels, departments, and branches. Allocate enough time to make real contact with select staff, so that you're not merely flitting through to make an impression.

Sometimes you can gain perspective by stepping back to get a detached overview of your organization. Vehicles for getting this kind of perspective include retreats, conferences, appropriate reading, working off-site, consulting with outsiders (consultants or peers), and comparison of current conditions and performance to that of other years or parallel organizations.

PLANNING FOR ACTION

Planning change means watching and adjusting your attack, looking for the opening, and sensing the prevailing rhythm so that you emerge victorious, or, in the case of managing, that you accomplish your goals. In the sixteenth century, renowned warrior Takeda Shingen wrote, as quoted in *Ideals of the Samurai,* "A man with deep far-sightedness will survey both the beginning and the end of a situation and continually consider its every facet as important."

Executives must manage change powerfully. But change puts a crimp in the smooth fabric of our routines; it's almost instinctive to stick with the status quo. We can't do that because the world continues to change; in fact, it takes an injection of energy just to remain at status quo. In many instances, managers have to plan as much to retain current market share as to achieve further growth.

Plan to defeat your real enemies. In an expert manager's case, these foes may be fear, resistance to change, self-centredness, or negative expectations about what staff are able to achieve; your adversaries are not dangerous people, but detrimental attitudes and practices. Find your enemies' strengths and weaknesses and plan your attack accordingly.

Planning is the first strategic step in taking action. It's not a substitute for action or movement, just a preparation for it. As Will Rogers said, "Planning gets you into things; hard work gets you out of them."

Courage is still needed; people may stand in place if they are too afraid of the risks in trying something new. Perhaps because of their own fear, many managers overplan, trying to account for every possible contingency. "If this situation arises we could do that; then if this happens, we can go with a or b; then again. . . ." Remember that strategizing never removes risk; taking action is always uncertain. But the risk involved in *not* moving or acting may be even greater. Not deciding, not moving are strategies, too, although they are ones that few managers would admit to choosing consciously.

In fact, there is a special danger in simply repeating the proven formulas from past experience instead of deciding to implement change. Martial arts instructor Frank Doran explains why he looks in the mirror every day and mentally washes off his old techniques. If he doesn't wash them off, Mr. Doran says, in twenty years he'll be performing yesterday's techniques. The world will have passed him by. Managers and organizations face this same danger.

At the work place, planning for change is basic self defence. In a rapidly changing world, pro-active planning prevents making yesterday's decisions today, and helps assure that the organization is current and able to compete.

If you start by looking at situations with fresh eyes, you will see openings. Walter Muryasz advises martial arts students to use "positive space" in defending against an attacker with a knife. New martial arts students focus too much on the weapon, he claims, so it appears, to the frightened defender, to be much larger than it really is. Mr. Muryasz points out, "The closer you pass by the weapon, the more control you have over it and the person who wields it." Advanced students see the positive space, the place where the weapon is not. With this focus, they can safely defend themselves from a thrusting knife or sword.

Positive spaces are "openings" (see chapter six). Black-belt managers also learn to focus on the positive space in the organization, spotting where change is possible or even welcomed. There are times when staff will try anything—especially when things have degenerated to a low level, when there is a "calm after the storm," or when you are wearing a halo after a recent accomplishment. At such times, there is room to manœuvre.

However, positive space is useless if you don't know where you are going. In any endeavour, your strategy should always spring from your mission, values, and goals. Black-belt manager John Fling knows this. As Loss Control Manager of a large port, John operates where there are complex, historically mistrustful relationships between the labour union and the management of companies served by the port. He uses position and timing to improve economic strength and reduce employee injuries in a work climate where "swords" are perpetually swinging. Sensitive to a long history of tension, he has instituted gradual and significant changes that helped heal mistrust between all parties, improved employee safety, and strengthened employer profitability.

DEFLECTING RESISTANCE TO CHANGE

The martial artist welcomes change as an ally. It is an opportunity to develop new skills. Change creates "room to move." Old obstacles may be shifted, and there is a new opportunity to work them out.

Much resistance to change is based on attitudes. No matter how remote an upcoming change is, the first thing people think is "how will it affect *me*?" Typically, people first look at the potentially negative effects on them and then they resist. But it is also possible that they will embrace positive elements of change. Understanding both can help you to package the change more attractively, and reduce resistance.

Different individuals have different appetites for change. Some drive home from work the same tried and true way; others find taking a different route refreshing. Certain people reposition their furniture every six months; they are often married to others who would rather the arrangement stay just as it is. Some remain in the same job for many years, but an increasing number move around between companies or within the same organization. Those who are less tolerant of change almost instinctively oppose any threat to the status quo.

Organizations that thrive on creating new products need to foster a climate of change. For example, change is the driving force in high-tech industries. "We are in the business of creating reality," as one manager of a multinational high-tech firm said. He also said, "The [corporate] culture here is never satisfied."

To promote this sense of urgency-for-change, some corporations have policies to ensure that their employees are neophilic (literally, change-loving). For instance, they hire fresh-out-of-school employees whom they see as being more hungry for innovation. (Many people assume that older people are more independent and resistant to change.) Such companies often have periodic reorganizations, whether they are needed or not. In addition to trying better to meet market demands, restructuring keeps employees slightly anxious; the company operates as if it believed that employees who are too content become complacent.

One high-tech company ranks performance reviews "on the curve." In other words, a certain percentage of employees in every department must be ranked below par. So an engineer who does excellent work for fifty-five hours each week (not uncommon in this industry) is given a substandard evaluation if department peers also work hard, but longer. There is a theory behind these anxiety-producing tactics. Although the corporation doesn't acknowledge it, I believe this system is designed to keep staff perpetually on edge so that they will continue to create.

When one technique always does the job, there may be little motivation to learn new ones. But in the high-tech field, yesterday's solution can mean rapid extinction. Just as there is nothing like a sound thrashing to get a martial artist working on new blocks and kicks, some companies believe that fear and anxiety forces greater creativity.

The high-tech company leaders may be partially correct. Generally, when things are going well and comfortably, the desire to change is reduced. The problem is that too much of anything can backfire. While it may be true that younger workers are fonder of innovation, they are also less stable, which may be a factor in burn-out or in loss of perspective. Moreover, a strong need for change can turn into career impatience, resulting in spin-off companies or job-hopping.

High stress levels bred by competitive performance reviews may translate into greater work drive, but in some staff it results in performance lowering worry. At one seminar, a staff engineer indicated he felt his company was anti-family. ("It's subtle, nothing they ever talk about, but it's there.") When he said this, most other people in the room nodded agreement.

As in the martial arts, balance—this time cultural—is the key. It is dangerous for staff to see the company as anti-family. By being overly change-oriented your organization may push out the very talented and creative people who can sustain real change. Finding and maintaining the balance is an art.

It's obvious that change is needed when an organization stops creating and becomes stagnant. In *The Tao of Jeet Kune Do,* Bruce Lee quoted Napoleon: "The art of government is not to let men grow stale." Rather, it is "an act of unbalancing." Remember, though, to seek balance in any unbalancing you do. Too much can have negative results. Plan on organizational change, but ask staff for their ideas. Shake them up positively, not just to make them uncomfortable. Reorganization can work well without jeopardizing morale.

You are not planning change to cause pain to people or to show your power to put strain on the organization. You want to influence the balance of the organization for the better, and to move it in a desirable direction. For example, the purpose of the advanced martial arts wrist lock techniques is *not* to cause pain or to twist a joint. By controlling the wrist, pressure is placed on the shoulder through the elbow which takes the opponent's balance. By taking someone's balance, you control him. Think of planning change in this light, as taking and moving the target's (department or individual) balance.

Participation is an important element in the acceptance of change. When employees feel involved in the decision-making, they have an investment in the solution. Master Nabeshima Naoshige is quoted in *Ideals of the Samurai:* "Encourage and listen well to the words of your subordinates. It is well known that gold lies hidden underground."

Many management books and seminars reinforce this, but so far the shift to more employee involvement in planning change is slow. Staff from the baby boom generation expect and want to give input into decisions that affect them. They have a unique and practical perspective that managers should not ignore. However, this doesn't mean going overboard and abdicating your responsibility; there are some managers who turn to participative planning as an easy way out—they feel little confidence in their own ability to plan and to make decisions. Management should still make the strategies and set direction, but with advice from the staff.

When changes are first discussed, there may be some expressions of emotional distress. Don't let employees' emotional reactions to change solidify into non-productive resistance. Harness those reactions to make the organization more efficient and stable. A case in point is one in which planning for change accomplished the "miraculous."

JOHN CHAPMAN: BLACK-BELT CHANGE MANAGER

Have you ever tried to manage people into happily working themselves out of jobs? Or persuaded staff to do what they consider impossible? John Chapman has. Armed with advanced planning techniques, he convinced a staff that had previously distrusted technology to embrace automation.

The Mapping Department of Portland General Electric manually processed increasing tides of information, to maintain a data base for other departments' billing, job planning, and service delivery monitoring.

Suburban sprawl continuously changed PGE's service area, and the maps had to be updated. Staff ranks swelled. Eventually, management decided that computerization might stem the increase in staff. Aesthetic illustrations would be replaced by data that could be generated quickly and accurately. But a significant investment in technology didn't produce the expected results. The technology-suspicious artists found it hard to change their values. Mappers resisted the new machines, and the result was a steadily mounting backlog of five years' work.

Chapman was assigned the project of making sure automation took hold with employees. First, he pinpointed why staff resisted the computerization. In their view, computers would jeopardize both their jobs and their way of life; peer communication and power patterns would be unbalanced. In addition, previously valued skills such as neat work habits would become the responsibility of a machine.

Next, he drafted a change management plan to eliminate within one calendar year the department's five-year backlog. Afterwards, a smaller staff would keep maps current. By the year's end, departmental productivity had risen three hundred percent; teamwork and morale had improved even as the staff was reduced by forty-seven percent. A project previously scheduled to take three years was completed in one, saving PGE $1.1 million. According to Chapman, "artists became information engineers" and the project was "a new learning experience for senior management."

How was this accomplished? Chapman used martial arts principles.

Clearing the field of battle. Knowing it is difficult to fight on two fronts, Chapman arrived at realistic change-over goals that upper-level management could accept and support.

Enlisting allies. He also met with mapping's internal clients to prioritize their information needs. Then he took his plan to existing mapping supervisors to invite their input and enlist their support.

Seeing the real enemies. Chapman realized his real "enemies" were the fear of job loss and change. He promised that no one would be laid off before the scheduled project completion date, even if it were finished early. He told staff that one of his main concerns was helping them protect and further their careers.

With his manager's support, he created the first performance incentive program within PGE. Staff helped determine the performance levels required for bonuses. The total cost of the incentive program was $103,000, compared to the $1.1 million saved.

Harnessing Do. The project was presented as an opportunity for transcending personal limitations. People were reminded to "be committed that [the plan] will work."

Defusing negative conflict. Prior to project start-up, Chapman hosted a staff meeting to explain fully the objectives of the project and the incentive program. Understanding that direct force creates further resistance, Chapman did not order compliance with project goals. Instead, he encouraged staff to respond honestly to the objectives outlined. He calmly responded to openly negative comments; he became "Rock, not water."

Managing morale. Understandably, pockets of low morale and performance surfaced during the project. Chapman combatted these by reminding staff that they had already accomplished the impossible. One mapper agreed, "My attitude for the first few months was 'there was no way.' Then we'd do it and I'd be excited. As soon as we started making our monthly objectives, morale really picked up."

Increasing team responsibility. Chapman encouraged a samurai "all for the team" ethic. He shifted task responsibility from individual employees to teams. Employees said that team support motivated higher performance. Accordingly, all incentives were paid for group, not personal performance.

Mr. Chapman also focused on results. He instituted flexible time, with emphasis on completion of tasks, rather than hours worked. Many chose to come in early when computers were more accessible and phones weren't ringing.

Focusing on personal development. He helped employees move from a "PGE owes you a job" to a "you are responsible for your own career" mentality. The department, he reaffirmed, would be cutting "positions, not people." He helped employees prepare themselves, meeting with each one to develop an individually tailored career marketing plan and resumé.

Fifteen out of thirty-two positions were terminated. Most of these employees found jobs within the utility at better pay; one became a consultant to the mapping industry. Another invented a device to speed up map delivery and quality control, which he intends to market independently.

In retrospect, the change-over was a powerful growth experience for most of the mapping staff. One employee reflected, "It was a good experience. Learning how to create our own jobs caused us to grow a lot. Since the project, people are a lot more gung ho." In addition to securing better positions and protecting their jobs, many staff learned how to become more responsible and more in control of themselves, manage change better, work together more successfully, and tap their inner power to go beyond what they thought were their limits. And John Chapman was recently promoted to general manager in the company.

THE UNBALANCED ORGANIZATION: CANDIDATE FOR CHANGE

A focused martial artist is one who strives for continual self-improvement, makes use of natural forces, and is dedicated to a higher purpose (do). A strong organization is defined by a common purpose, effective internal communication between parts, and a willingness to co-operate.

When he is progressing and learning, change helps the martial artist continue to grow; when he becomes stagnant or disillusioned, change can help get him out of a rut.

Similarly, organizational change may be needed in two instances: as a prescription for a troubled organization or as a means of strengthening a basically sound one. It's important to know when the corporation is edging onto threatening territory. There are some specific danger signs of an unbalanced organization.

First, people lose focus. Employees disregard the mission or become confused about their goals. They become too concerned with the short-term (for example, quarterly profits) at the expense of longer-term planning. They don't monitor the marketplace. There is too much emphasis on status. People spend much more energy on covering themselves than on seeking creative solutions to problems.

Interdepartmental rivalries get out of hand. People lose the ability to communicate or co-operate. They put each other down or engage in scapegoating, refuse to share vital information, try to make points at other departments' expense, don't talk with those in other departments, or feel more allegiance to their own department or division than to the organization as a whole.

Morale breaks down. People are chronically unhappy. Turnover increases; they pine for the "good old days" and rush to leave at the end of their day, or talk only about their time off.

Emotional outbursts surface. There may be screaming incidents, door slamming, episodes of throwing things, or even attacks on co-workers.

No one of these signs is cause for alarm. But when several occur in tandem, or one persists, this may indicate the organization has entered the danger zone. Strong remedial action is needed.

THINKING—AND NOT THINKING—STRATEGICALLY

The martial artist believes it is better to deal with reality than fantasy; he knows there will be always be up periods and down periods. What do you do when you get hit, or when major problems occur unexpectedly? This isn't the time for recriminations. When he sees a student berating himself for missing a block, Walter Muryasz teaches, "The attack begins at this point. While you're criticizing yourself for getting punched, your opponent will hit you several more times. Instead, imagine you're practising a specific defence, one that begins after just being hit once. Martial arts don't make you invincible; you may get hit. Just don't add to your own problems by blanking out. Do the best you can with what is presented to you."

From the standpoint of taking action, the problem really begins whenever you first notice it. It makes little sense to dwell on the "should-have-dones" and "why-didn'ts." When you're in trouble, blaming and fantasizing will only allow matters to progress along a destructive path while you waste time and energy that could redirect the organization onto safer ground. So when you hear of an exodus of talented people, ask "What has been going on?" and "What has been tried and what hasn't?" and "What can we do now to stem the tide?" rather than "Why wasn't I informed sooner?" or "Why didn't you do something about this?"

Chinese martial master Lun Yu is quoted in *Ideals of the Samurai:* "Making a mistake and not correcting it, this is a real mistake." So, after you take care of the immediate major threat, go back and correct the underlying organization problems—which probably include inadequate monitoring and poor communication flow.

Through planning, you can most clearly discern your immediate needs; those of a few months ahead are less distinct, and the requirements of the distant future are even less clear. When you make long-term plans don't carve them in stone. Because conditions will change, so should your plans accordingly. Periodically review and readjust long-range plans. Have market conditions changed? Are you still on target? Should the goals be adjusted?

On the other hand, some managers don't set goals because they think "Why bother? Everything's in a state of flux." Besides sounding like an excuse, this attitude can result in haphazard actions; you may not be moving toward your organizational mission.

Without goals, managers feel more reactive, and "manage by crisis." They are like those fighters who are always on the defensive, blocking this thrust and parrying that one. Typically, without any offence (i.e., your plan), a blow eventually lands and the fighter is knocked out.

Naturally, while you are planning, you still have to meet present needs—keep your unit functioning smoothly and serving your customers. In real life, planning takes time, but it pays back dividends. Some tips can help.

- Make sure you're not rushing yourself. Musashi noted, "Immature strategy is the cause of grief." Remember to take time in your planning—solicit a range of initial input, make calm decisions, and get feedback on your strategy.

- Use Bruce Lee's advice: "Set patterns, incapable of adaptability, of pliability, only offer a better cage. Truth is outside of all patterns." Think creatively, with the past as an indicator, not as a predictor. Some of the most expensive planning mistakes managers make come from the notion that "what happened before will happen again." Past experience is not wholly reliable in a changing world.

- Create planning rituals, similar to martial arts' kata (a fighting form against invisible opponents). Have a planning day or meeting with a suitable name ("Mission in the Future Day," "Smart Strategies," etc.). Meet at the same locale at the same approximate time each year. Involve all necessary staff in some portion of the planning process even if just to gather ideas.

- Use your corporate mission statement in planning. Review it and use it to set goals and to help staff become rededicated.

- Bigger isn't always better. Enlarging a business, like inflating a balloon, can also stretch organizational flaws. *Before* expansion—branching out, franchising, etc.—is the time to solve small but important corporate problems and set necessary precedents. Smaller organizations are usually easier to control; and communication flows more easily.

DEVELOPING RHYTHM

"The Way of strategy is the Way of nature," Musashi said. "When you appreciate the power of nature, knowing the rhythm of any situation, you will be able to do anything you wish."

Rhythm is crucial in the martial arts. Michel Random wrote, in *The Martial Arts*, "Every movement is a rhythm, just as in painting, music or poetry. If one is aware of the rhythm, it is possible to sense what is in the rhythm and what is not. This new sense would be like a spontaneous master if only one were to heed it. A correct rhythm expresses proportion, balance, universal order. Rhythms reveal whether they are in conjunction or in opposition to each other. Work on rhythms is already a rule of life and in itself an understanding of harmony and discord."

Paul Maslak put it even more poetically: "You yield to your opponent's slightest pressure and stick to him at his slightest retreat. The rhythm of your movements is kept in constant time with your opponent's. You are like water, rushing into his every weakness and ebbing from his every strength, until he has drowned himself in his own actions."

Look for favourable organizational rhythms when planning—when competitors are weaker (maybe they're regrouping), when employees appear more receptive to change (a big contract has raised morale), or when there is an opening (capital becomes freer). Sense when employees would welcome a period of faster, or slower change.

Roger Graybeal heads a statewide chapter of the Automobile Club of America, and has applied his martial arts training to developing managerial rhythm. His predecessor was a highly controlling manager who exerted authority over his mid-level managers' smallest decisions. Consequently, these managers became conditioned to checking in before they acted. But Roger knows that in these times, no one person can make all the decisions in a middle-sized organization. To get the most out of people you must allow them to act. His change involved retraining his staff in initiative. But how can you develop a new rhythm in a hesitant, yet able management team?

His staff was ready for change, so Roger made the most of this receptivity. Although he is interested in swift movement, Roger exercised patience and a fine sense of timing to control the pace of change. First, he set the stage so that management and employees would look forward to the coming changes. Then he employed a gradual, penetrating approach: "This will take some time, but within two years, we will create a newly vitalized organization." Benefits were improved; salaries were raised; there were more promotional opportunities. Although the staff had some anxiety about the changes, morale rose. Still, Roger is watching and adjusting his strategy to guide his Automobile Club into an efficient, profitable, service organization.

BALANCING FORCES IN PLANNING

To the martial artist, life is a matter of movement and energy.

The physical view of the world applies to business. People and organizations exist in a magnetic-like force field, according to Kurt Lewin, a social scientist. Forces act on them in each moment. Nothing ever stays the same. When they do seem to be constant, there is actually a state of "dynamic equilibrium." For example, look at the production level of any assembly team. This level does not remain constant, it fluctuates within narrow limits. Lewin would say this pattern persists because there is a balance between the forces that encourage higher productivity and those that lower it.

Advance planning allows you to adjust the balance of forces with relatively little effort; it also provides for lasting changes.

How to do a Force Field Analysis:

1. Decide upon a pattern you wish to change, for example, the productivity level of clerical staff. Draw a line representing this current level.

2. Draw an arrow pushing up against the line for each "driving force" that tends to increase clerical productivity. Examples include physical factors (soft lighting, ergonomic chairs, comfortable temperature), supervisory influences (close monitoring of work, group quality circle meetings), organizational factors (relatively high pay, incentives for performance). Draw each arrow so its length reflects the relative strength of each force.

3. Similarly, draw an arrow pushing down against the line for each productivity-reducing "restraining force." These, too, include physical factors (inadequate working space, distracting noise), supervisory influences (overmonitoring, too much time spent in meetings), and organizational factors (inadequate or poorly conducted training, little say in decision-making, long work periods without breaks).

Note that the same force can be deemed both negative *and* positive, propelling productivity to a point and hampering it past that point. Take, for example, a concerned supervisor. Employees might work hard for her; but her tendency to do too much for them prevents their learning from mistakes, and thus puts a lid on potential increases in productivity. Noise level can be a force for both increasing excitement and distracting from work. Perception and experience will help you allocate forces according to their real influence on productivity.

There are two approaches to raising the "line of productivity" where the driving and restraining forces meet. Either push harder from underneath by adding more driving forces, or reduce forces that block movement to a higher level.

Changes that occur from adding forces don't produce lasting results. As discussed in chapter five, "pushing" adds force to the system, making it more stressful and less stable. So when you change by adding more driving forces (e.g., more monitoring of clerical work), productivity goes up for a time, but returns soon to a lower level.

Black-belt managers prefer the second approach to raising productivity. This involves isolating and reducing forces that restrain people from doing the job. For example, you may decide to reduce distracting noise, hold shorter meetings, shorten work periods without breaks. As force is removed, a more stable, less stressful system is created, at a higher production level. Studies have shown that this approach brings lasting improvements with less resistance.

Some creative thinking may be needed to discover ways to reduce the strength of a force. For instance, if you decide excessive noise is a restraining force, you might provide each worker with ear plugs, install sound absorbing walls, or move the entire department to a quieter area.

Experienced martial artists prefer to parry, not block the force of an incoming blow. Stopping a punch cold can injure the blocking arm because a lot of force is absorbed in a small area. More important, the energy behind a strong attack cannot be checked outright; directly blocking a punch actually triggers the opponent's other hand to strike, or foot to spin kick. It's better to safely play out the force, extending it to where it is of no danger to you.

With this in mind, plan to adjust and reduce blocking forces, not stop them cold. Are you concerned about a strong cafeteria rumour mill? Trying to block it will induce a second-hand attack of increased gossip and rumours. You can reduce the strength of the cafeteria grapevine by giving out more information and by openly responding to serious concerns.

When applied insightfully, Force Field Analysis is a proven, high-leverage technique for planning change. With all the forces influencing the level of productivity, how do you know which ones to weaken? Where do you focus to institute change?

Make sure to include all relevant forces in your planning model so your analysis accurately reflects the workplace. When you have recognized these, look to change restraining forces that are

1. *Most influential*. It's like taking on the leader in a group attack; defeat him and others may fall into line. Interview and observe your employees. What most gets in their way? What do they continually complain about?

2. *Easiest to control*. In other multiple attack situations, it's preferable to go after the weakest attacker, using him as a shield against the others. You may not have the power to reduce low pay rates as a blocking force. If so, focus elsewhere. In general, put your efforts where they can most realistically make a difference. Experience will point the way.

SMALL CHANGES CAN MAKE BIG DIFFERENCES

If you try to hold down the wrist of a strong person, he will probably still be able to raise his arm with ease. Even if you use two hands to press down, you may not succeed; even if you can, you'll probably not be able to keep his arm down for very long before you tire. But, if you think like a martial artist and use leverage, you will approach this challenge differently. Now, you will hold down on his fingertips. By directing your force just six inches away from the wrist, you can immediately increase your control, effortlessly preventing the strongest person from lifting his arm.

Impatience and lack of discipline often undermine the changes people plan. Whether it comes to mastering the martial arts, accruing wealth, getting into shape, or losing weight, many attempt to succeed overnight. Doing too much too quickly usually leaves them injured or uncomfortable, and not much better off.

With this in mind, warrior Nabeshima Naoshige wrote, "Coming up in the world should be done in the same way as ascending a stairway." Making incremental changes is like climbing stairs. Eventually you progress rapidly, but, in the beginning of a change, make sure to hit every step. If the changes are made step-by-step, they will *seem* "slow enough" and less shocking to staff.

In contrast, changes done by leaps are more stressful, harder to sustain, and make you more vulnerable. In planning, after all, there's no guarantee your strategy will be correct. At least if you're proceeding in increments, you can assess your results and adjust as needed. Employ leverage by planning small changes that make large differences. Search for low-stress steps that move you toward your goal.

There are plenty of examples from everyday life. To get in shape, you can start by exercising for five minutes, three times each week. How can you not spare five minutes? But if you set your sights at a half hour daily, it's easy to find reasons to avoid working out. At the lower level, you're using the "natural" feeling of guilt for, not against you. Those who try to get in shape in one weekend often only succeed in getting injured.

To lose weight, think of doing it gradually. Taking off half a pound each week will result in twenty-six pounds that stay off. And, all things remaining equal, you can reduce by this amount relatively easily. There are approximately 3500 calories in a pound of fat; lower your food intake by 1750 calories by forgoing extra portions of dessert three times each week. The key is to make small changes consistently.

In business, supermarkets generally run on a one to three percent net profit margin. They're profitable by making that small percentage over many sales.

Similarly, the black-belt executive plans to leverage small changes into large organizational gains. Incremental, unthreatening, step-by-step changes are less likely to be resisted.

Smaller changes can also be more motivating. As John Chapman contends, "It has to be perceived by individual employees that goals are within their reach." Large projects usually contain easily recognizable interim periods that can serve as attainable milestones. These are appropriate times to assess problems, make "steering decisions" (what to modify), and celebrate progress toward the overall goal. By employing an incremental approach to change, you can even strengthen an approval-seeking employee by giving him small tasks that increasingly exercise his independence.

Strategy is an advanced art, one that black-belt managers train a long time to master. Like all martial abilities, good strategy comes from self control. Taisen Deshimaru wrote, in *The Zen Way to the Martial Arts,*

In a martial arts tournament, it is impossible to maintain the same intensity of concentration indefinitely. At some point the attention wavers and we show a fault, a *suki,* an opportunity which the opponent [is] able to seize.

This question of opportunity arises in every contest, however, not just in the martial arts—in argument, business . . .

You must not show your weak points, either in the martial arts or in everyday life. Life is a fight!

Plan, then act to make change happen, and you will win your most important fights.

The Martial Art of Strategy—Planning To Achieve Change: Techniques for Action

- In planning strategy, be able to answer employees' question, "How will it affect me?"

- How strong is your current position? Assess your position in terms of market conditions, competitors, employee morale. What would you like to see changed? What are your staff's present abilities and attitudes toward change?

- See the positive space in any planning situation. In the unit for which you're responsible, where is there the most room to manœuvre?

- Remember that strategy can show amazing results.

- Watch your planning "balance." Do enough, but not too much, contingency planning.

- Assess your own style. Let go of what you do just out of habit. Create space for improvement.

- Look at participation as a gauge of staff acceptance of change. Think of ways to involve staff in the planning.

- If you "get hit" during a change, don't stop for recriminations. Keep going. You'll have time to lick your wounds later, and think of ways to prevent similar blows.

- In any situation, see the counterbalancing forces—stability and movement; risk and return.

- Think of planning as a ongoing process, not a one-time event. First you plan, then act, monitor, adjust, and replan.

- Sense the rhythms of change in your organization. Does it have spurts of movement followed by months-long lulls? Or are steady gradual improvements more common? Decide whether to attempt to work within or change these cycles.

- Assess forces at play by the use of Force Field Analysis.

- For stable change, reduce restraining forces.

- Direct, don't attempt to stop, strong blocking forces.

- Make a change implementation plan; break down the steps into small, easily attainable milestones.

CHAPTER NINE

Becoming An Agent of Change

It can be said that the martial artist is in harmony when he has learned to adapt and flow with change, which is the nature of the Universe. He is at one with all when this adaptation and flow are an unconscious part of himself—when it can be said of him that he is change itself.

Walter Muryasz, Precepts of the Martial Artist

To know and to act are precisely the same.

Samurai maxim

THE BLACK-BELT AGENT OF CHANGE

Martial arts experts are agents of change. Through understanding how to change themselves, they change others. This takes an understanding of relative position. The opponent reacts to my action; almost simultaneously, I react to his. As I move to the left, he twists left. The black belt leads in this dance of change.

Hapkido, jujitsu, judo, aikido, and others are among the most difficult of martial arts to learn. They teach one how to control another's balance. They require sensitivity to slight shifts of balance, and making small changes in relative position, angle, or pressure. Push on a person in one position, at a certain angle, and he may be rock solid; shift an inch to the side, and now just a few pounds of pressure can easily dislodge him.

Think like a judo expert, and become an agent of change. "Agent for change" is my term for someone who causes or helps institute positive change. It is knowing the conditions and susceptibility to movement. Many try it, but few are skilled. Remember the inertia principle: a body at rest tends to remain at rest; a body in motion tends to remain in motion. On water, a push easily moves a boat; much greater force won't budge it on dry land. Helping others make desired changes is truly an ability of a black-belt manager.

Many managers live by the Rule of Effort: "The harder I try, the more I will accomplish." Perhaps, but sometimes they get in their own way by trying too hard to make something happen, as this classic martial arts story shows.

A young man approached the house of a great swordsmaster and asked, "Sir, I yearn to be a great swordsman. How long would it take me if I practised every day?"

The master looked him over and replied, "Ten years."

"Sir, what if I practised at night also?"

"Twenty years," answered the master.

"And if I lived with the sword, slept with it, dedicated my very existence to it?"

"Thirty years," smiled the master and turned away.

Instead of forcing change by over-exertion, use martial arts principles that make changing easier. For instance, martial artists create a "soft spot" in their opponent's concentration by the distraction of screaming. Distraction works in other areas, too. For instance, have you ever tried to change lanes and had another driver speed up to prevent your moving in front of him? If you look toward a different lane, and let him see you do this, he will usually back off; now, he no longer will feel you're a threat to cut him off. When the space opens, quickly and smoothly change lanes.

Martial artists and managers focus on restoring balance. Changing, like walking, is a process of risk and recovery. Knowing that change is always stressful and brings some degree of resistance, how do you help individuals survive it, work more productively and efficiently as a team, and adapt to, or even welcome, new systems?

Mentor Graphics' senior manager Ron Swingen says, "Managers of change—that's what we are for each other. And the only way for people to learn and create is in an environment where mistakes are not punished. There are actions that might produce catastrophic results, and we've got to put safeguards into place, like 'check with me before you act.' "

Shearson's Karen Nish says, "I never forget that dealing with change means dealing with people. Helping them manage change strengthens our business."

John Chapman contends, "Employees can improve their productivity by over fifty percent if [they] were better managed."

SETTING THE CLIMATE OF CHANGE

The martial tradition recognizes that underlying intent is crucial. The Japanese speak of "the sword that kills" and "the sword that preserves life." Both swords are sharp and both are used in battle. But the "sword that kills" is wielded by someone prone to violence, one who plots revenge or fights solely for personal gain. In contrast, the more enviable "sword that preserves life" belongs to one who, during a fight, uses only as much force as is necessary and no more, defending himself calmly, without anger, without thought of retribution.

Remember the importance of intention should the time come for you to plan layoffs or to fire a subordinate. Work at controlling yourself. Drop feuds—having organizational enemies requires too much energy. Let go of anger. Don't expose yourself foolishly, but when you must sever a relationship, choose the "sword that preserves life." Make your cuts with calmness and caring.

Black-belt managers emphasize creating the right climate, a nonthreatening and productive one where resistance to change is reduced. Managers who are skilled agents of change trust colleagues and employees by giving them relevant information and by believing they will do well. And they are trustworthy themselves, maintaining honest relationships, and following through with their promises.

Karen Nish has flown to many cities for Shearson to integrate new brokerage houses into her company. Her strategy? "I live with them for a while, get to know them, and let them get to know me. Then, when the relationship has become less threatening and more personal, I sit and talk with them and explain, 'This is what the division expects.' The biggest thing is getting to know the people and getting them to trust you."

TAKING BALANCE

Moving any person can be difficult. You can try to drag someone along by the wrist; she may grimace, take the pain, and shift away, or hit you in spite of the discomfort. Push a person from the side, and she may twist away to evade the force.

When a person is standing in any position, there are eight *kuzushi* (unbalance) points on the floor, close to his feet. Get him to lean over one of these points and he will lose the ability to deliver significant physical power. This is called "disturbing" someone's balance. Apply downward pressure at this time—as little as fifteen pounds will do on the strongest man—and he will fall. This "breaks" his balance.

The easiest way to accomplish this is to control a person's centreline. A martial artist who understands this centreline principle will be able to move the largest attacker wherever she wants him.

Think of a person as an upright, almost cylindrical shape. The easiest way to move the "cylinder" is to push through its middle. Because the object is not completely round, its centreline, running from top to bottom of the object, will shift away. You have to follow it and keep pushing down through its middle. A ten-pound push through the centre of a linebacker will guide him wherever you want, whereas he can shrug off one hundred pounds of force that is off his centreline.

To move an organization, first determine where its centreline is. It runs through the middle of the organization, through its head (upper management), its heart (middle management), abdomen (line staff), and legs (support staff). Determine who is on the periphery and who is on the centreline. Experience and observation will help you determine where the centreline is in any department. Departments have their own centreline, located in natural leaders and crucial staff through whom work and communication flow. Other staff gravitate toward these people.

Control the centreline and you have the power of position. Concentrate your efforts on those in the centreline; the rest of the organization will come along.

CREATING INDEPENDENT AGENTS OF CHANGE

Martial masters point to the number of their black-belt students with pride. The more highly skilled people a master has developed, the more honour he accrues. Expand your sphere of influence; train people to be black-belt agents of change. Then you won't have to do it all yourself.

Sometimes the way to support someone is to not be there to support him at all. Don Angier calls this principle "The Void." During the middle of throwing someone there is a time to position yourself in one of his kuzushi spots. When he subsequently leans on you, vanish, so he falls into the space you just occupied.

Similarly at work, there's a time to disappear and let the people who are committed to doing the work be on their own. In certain situations, you know they're positioned and ready to go, they've succeeded with a similar job before, but they *just don't have the confidence* to complete the project. Rather than letting them remain dependent on you, let them fall into a stronger spot.

Tell them, "I know you can do it." Give more guidelines if you wish, then disappear. If they come to you for help, don't make necessary decisions for them. Place the decision back in their lap. ("Could you take care of this, and keep me apprised?") You can even plan to be unavailable for a short time.

But soon after, restore the balance by getting back to them. Help them achieve a new level of learning by reviewing what has happened and what they have learned. Foster independence for high-level functioning.

Karen Nish says, "My managers have to be independent. I give them a lot of support, but realistically they have to be able to make decisions on their own. With new managers, I never criticize their decisions unless they're jeopardizing the firm or costing us money. I can give them alternatives and forecast probable consequences, but they've got to develop their own style. I give them all the tools and all the guidance, but I never tell them who to hire or how to deal with changes in their office."

Like martial arts experts, black-belt managers have to be able to recover after a mistake. IBM founder Tom Watson, Sr., did. One of his managers made a critical decision that cost the company a million dollars. The manager offered Watson his resignation. "Let's not hear more of this," Mr. Watson said. "We just spent $1 million training you." Change managers employ mistakes as teaching devices. And if the error is large enough, it will create a lasting memory.

In the martial tradition, teaching is a part of learning. It helps the instructor as much as or more than the student. It's common to see a brown belt or even a lower ranked student lead a portion of class. Students who know teach those who know less. Similarly, Karen Nish has her managers consult with newly acquired branches. She says everyone benefits. "They work really hard, but they enjoy being the outside expert. What they learn in doing this makes them better at their own branches, too."

THE POWER OF CONNECTION

Have you ever observed a martial arts class? Martial artists frequently bow—upon entering and leaving the training hall, to the picture of the master, the instructor, and to each other before practice or sparring.

This *reigi* (courtesy) is more than Oriental politeness. It is practise in staying calm and making contact. To fight well, you must make real contact with the other person. How can you read a changing situation if you are disconnected or preoccupied by your own thoughts?

Making contact is the first step in helping others change. Experience feeling connected to them. See things from their perspective. I have never seen someone change another positively without this empathy.

Takeda Nobushige explained, "If one is dealing with a weak and powerless person, he should handle that person as though handling water. When dealing with the powerful and mighty, he should use the same respect as when handling fire."

WHAT MAKES IT HARDER TO CHANGE?

As in the martial arts, successful agents of change don't go about their work haphazardly. They understand both the smooth parts of their path and the obstacles. This way they can successfully traverse more of the former and avoid the latter. There are some specific obstacles that all managers must avoid.

Too much stress can make it hard to tolerate and learn from change.

Lack of support from others and outright obstructionism are the tactics of threatened people. Be cautious of people who are jealous or easily threatened in any organization. They may not be thinking in terms of mutual benefit, only about blocking change.

Have you ever gone to a seminar or read a book and been charged up about changes you wished to instil? Then you found others downplaying your insights. ("Never work here. Pie in the sky.") Typically, they are passing their own negative attitudes over to you.

Poor attitude/self-image can make tearing a paper bag an overwhelming task, while the right attitude can help you shatter stones. I once taught an underconfident student to take lengthy "projection rolls." (Such rolls are an important skill for self-protection on a crowded training mat.) He dove over one, then two, then three crouched students. I stopped him, and asked him to repeat this three more times. The first two went quite well. Then, in mid-air on his last roll, something came over his face. For some reason, he lost all confidence, and with it, his control. He fell heavily and poorly, bruising himself. A failure of attitude short-circuited his repetition of a recent success. We talked about this incident afterwards. It became a strong learning experience for us both.

Right attitudes are just as significant for organizations as for self development.

If your organization has a loser attitude ("We'll be one of the ones analysts are projecting will go belly-up; we just can't adapt"), work toward helping the staff think of themselves positively. Give recognition to excellent adaptations of techniques or processes at work. Reformat your mission so it is clearly future-oriented, and make strategic use of internal public relations (newsletters, the names of company recreational teams).

Another kind of attitude/image problem is mixed feelings; that is, a part of an individual or an organization doesn't want to change. Acknowledge and accept these feelings—fighting them only makes them stronger—then provide the information and assurance required to reduce ambiguity and threat.

Lack of awareness of the benefits to staff may result in resistance. Why would anyone pay the price of the bruises and the time required, unless they saw the benefits of martial arts practice? People usually don't have any problem seeing the costs of change, so it's natural that they'll tend to dislike a change when they can't see its benefits.

Let them know specifically how they will benefit from the change. If you can't see any benefits for them, don't expect staff to buy the change.

Inertia is the greatest obstacle to change. Many people would rather stay set in their ways. You've got to get them moving in some direction, any direction. This is the essence of motivation (see chapter five).

An unsupportive physical environment discourages especially the inexperienced. The training hall is designed to help the martial artist grow psychologically and physically. When he is skilled enough, he can thrive anywhere; any place can be his training hall. But in the beginning, environmental support can make a needed difference.

Let's say you wish to break a habit like smoking. If all your friends also smoke, there is a lot of pressure to continue; and going to smoky places—bars, bowling alleys, bridge clubs—can make it even more difficult to quit.

In organizations, inappropriate environments can negate the momentum for change. Environments do affect communication. For instance, movement to a team orientation can be dissipated by meeting in a hall where the chairs are fixed in rows or in a boardroom with long tables. So choose your meeting rooms and their set-up with care.

Uncertainty and waiting can erode the protective calmness that is necessary for approaching change effectively. It's a lot easier to defend yourself when you know from when and where the attack is going to come. I recall being the *uke* (attacker in martial arts, literally, "one who is thrown") in a well-attended demonstration. The instructor was showing the finer points of a high hip throw. He parried my attack, took me over his hip and *held me there,* while he explained technique to the group. I knew that at some point he would complete the throw with some force. Waiting was difficult; I had to will myself to relax and be ready. It was a lot easier to take the same falls when he demonstrated the same technique at full speed.

For many people, not knowing can be worse than knowing the worst. I have asked managers in seminars, "Would you rather be told 'Your position will definitely be eliminated at the end of the year' or 'There's a fifty-fifty chance you'll be laid off'?" Most say they'd rather hear the first. The uncertainty makes them feel less in control, even though they may keep their job. ("If I know I'll be leaving, I can plan for it. If I have a chance to stay, I wouldn't know whether to job hunt or not.")

It's possible to reduce fear of the unknown by keeping people abreast of information related to the change. Share your battle plans, at least the broad strategy. The specifics may be inappropriate. Ironically, you can reduce some anxiety by letting staff know when you're uncertain: "We hope not to have further layoffs, but this will depend on how strong the dollar is and other factors. We'll let you know as soon as we ourselves know."

When an organization faces technological change, it's especially important that the staff know what's coming and what results are expected. Next, providing them with strong training can help the new technology appear less intimidating. When employees have the time and opportunity to develop skills gradually in a non-threatening climate, resistance disappears.

WHAT MAKES IT EASIER TO CHANGE?

Support by management is as important as that of peers. The samurai knew the power of team support. The change agent knows that change in any group should be supported by management or else the group will be the target of mistrust from others within the organization. In other words, be wary of creating a "renegade" department. If the changing department is truly serving the organization's needs, top management should acknowledge its work. This way you enlist the ripple effect. Ideally, change should start with the policy-making body and spread down. In a department, it is the supervisor or manager.

Reinforcement from managers prompts further changes. Whenever possible, support requests for change that come from within the ranks. These overtures place you in a responding position; so employees will feel pushed less. Needless to say, resistance will be reduced. A good suggestion program can generate many requests for positive changes.

The agent of change knows he can succeed by getting department staff to think as a team. I have developed programs that apply martial arts methods to reduce falling and back injuries at work. In our seminars, we emphasize "playing team defence." We remind employees that even safety is a team effort; in sports the best team wins by playing team defence. Cover for your co-workers, help them stay injury-free; they will do the same for you. People respond to this approach enthusiastically.

Supportive physical environments enhance the prospects for change. Poll staff on the environmental changes they believe will improve productivity.

Timely positive feedback is needed by those experiencing change, especially those with low task maturity. This is one of the main reasons the belt colour system was instituted. In many traditional martial arts, there were no belt ranks. To sustain their students' efforts and confidence, instructors began to award coloured belts. As he moves up through the ranks, the beginning martial artist feels reassured he is progressing. In a sense, belt promotions are milestones.

Changing takes effort and things usually don't progress linearly; often it is "three steps forward, two steps back." The master or the manager shouldn't let positively changing staff become discouraged. He lets them know how well they've done. Staff's self-motivation recharge when they see progress; success is probably the best attitude setter.

Fear of sticking with the old can motivate change. Many people begin martial arts study because they're afraid of being attacked. But they usually move beyond this self-defence motivation very quickly.

Smart change managers see their role as making sure their people succeed with change. When a person, or an organization, realizes the old ways no longer work, they look for a way out. Don't wait for them to try anything out of desperation. ("We're losing money? Let's cut our sales staff. We're paying out too much to them anyway.") Provide them with ways of changing that have good chances of success.

HELPING THE RESISTIVE TO CHANGE

Mature martial artists have to be able to deal with strong-minded attackers. Not everyone surrenders easily. Managers also frequently work with change-resistant people. After all, individuals have varying levels of tolerance for change. When they feel their organization has asked too much, some staff will dig in their heels.

For example, engineers tend not to like change, says Ron Swingen. "They are taught laws and models that are supposed to be fixed. As a group, engineers don't like deviations of any sort, in people, systems, or machines. Not only that, they are geared to work on their own. Yet so much of our work is team project-based. I try continually to help them see change as an ally, not necessarily as an enemy, and to provide models of people who've made successful changes in their personal as well as professional lives."

And any industry that has been relatively static may have more than its share of security-conscious (often the same as change-resistant) staff. Suddenly, these people are told that the old ways of doing things are now inadequate and they must change. Managers in such industries face a distinct challenge from those resistant to change. A good example is the field of health care. The industry has been changing rapidly after a long period of stability, and many health care professionals are concerned with professional security as well as quality of patient care. There are also many external and regulatory pressures. On top of these, competition has become ferocious. In this climate, staff acceptance of change is crucial to the very survival of their health care organization.

To move a resisting opponent toward change, shift his balance. This is a momentary move; it doesn't mean attempting to *keep* a person "on his toes" or uncomfortable. Besides creating ill will, this would take tremendous effort and control to sustain.

Instead, *disturb* the resistant staff member's balance and then, as quickly as practical, guide him into a position of better balance. Just as there are eight kuzushi points around the body, people have emotional "change points." Resistance is a symptom that one of these points is exposed; it can signal both loss of emotional balance and fear. A person usually braces because he is afraid of being pushed over by some threatening force. By stiffening and leaning into it, he hopes to avoid getting hurt (ironically, bracing doesn't work against superior force). On the other side, someone who is sure of her strength and position won't stiffen against an attack. She knows that staying relaxed and fluid will help her move more effectively.

There are also some individuals who are not just inert resisters, but very strong, dangerous obstructors. When attacked by such a strong opponent, be careful not to get hurt. You also want to avoid injury to bystanders or to the attacker himself. (In chapter six, it was noted that protecting others requires a high level of expertise.)

Three Steps to Create Movement

Think of judo, in which a person's own resistance can be used to break his inertia and get him moving. This approach also applies to individual employees, departments, and entire organizations. For example, you may decide that a subordinate has become ineffective in one important area. He needs to quickly improve but has a history of resisting change efforts. What can you do? Disturb his stability *by creating movement* and channel him toward the desired change.

Think of this as a three-step process. You have a heavy block of ice in the doorway and you want to move it to a better place. First, melt the ice. Then channel the water where you wish it. Third, refreeze it so it stays in place.

Step 1: Melting/"Unfreezing" Strategies

"Melting" means separating an opponent or resistant employee from the strength of an entrenched position that needs changing. Some Chinese martial arts techniques do this by "uprooting," or lifting the opponent's feet from the ground.

It may seem easiest to neutralize any attacker—or fire an uncooperative employee—without regard to other consequences. But firing someone is a waste of a potentially valuable resource and should never be a strategy of first resort. Firing is expensive when you consider the costs of replacement, lowered productivity, unemployment compensation, and even wrongful discharge suits. Also, arbitrarily firing staff will be seen as unreasonable and will result in increased resistance and lower morale among those who remain. Moreover, what do you do when there are several resistive employees? You can't very well fire them all.

Turn up the heat on resistive employees to detach them from accustomed, yet useless ways. You want to instil doubt about the old approach and get them to consider change. There are some things to keep in mind when doing this.

Failure can be harnessed and put to good use. In *Zen in the Art of Archery,* the author asks why the archery master had looked on so long at the student's futile efforts to draw the bow correctly, and had not taught him the necessary breath control technique right away.

A senior student remarked, "Had he begun the lessons with the breathing exercises, he would never have been able to convince you that you owe anything decisive to them. You had to suffer shipwreck through your own efforts before you were ready to seize the lifebelt he threw you." Sometimes things have to get so bad that the person is ready to abandon his old approach. Be prepared to seize the moment when the resistant "target" is frustrated by failure. Rather than crowing, "I told you so," offer a better way.

Timing, as in the example above, is essential. For instance, one of the best times to promote safe practices is just after an injury. Treat the accident as a melting experience. Approach this with sensitivity. ("We were all sorry to hear of this. I know we thought this couldn't happen here. What's done is done. But at least we can learn from John's accident.")

Sometimes you have to help a resistive employee see that her ways are unsuccessful. Call her in for a talk. Remind yourself of the purpose of the meeting, beforehand. Don't let yourself launch a personal attack; the employee will likely rationalize that away. ("I'm fine, we just have a personality conflict," or "She has it in for me.") Mentally set your attitude. Is this the time to be wood or steel?

Clearly show the resistant person how ineffective her approach has been by having specific documentation. ("You missed deadlines on March 23, April 9, and April 15.") You may then want to ask her to comment on the documentation and to suggest improvements. Be prepared for denial and resistance. This is a good time to be steel— flexible, but firm.

Wise managers have learned that some people have higher melting points. If the employee still doesn't get the idea that her ways need changing, you may have to further turn up the heat by enlisting your boss. When both of you meet with the employee, she's less likely to dismiss it as a personality conflict.

In some cases, you may wish to confront her carefully at a meeting. Be calm in your descriptions. Don't make a martyr of her. Talk less about her ("You really screwed up again.") and more about the approach or actions ("That method has again failed to get the desired results. What can we do?"). It's best if another employee is prepared to support your perception of the actions.

Sometimes, resistive people support each other; this group may launch a counter-offensive against positive changes. Weaken these social supports. Such conspiratorial cabals are no more beneficial to their members than they are to their colleagues or to the organization.

It's tempting to squelch such groups with the heavy-handed use of managerial power—transfers and firing. But once again a forced, authoritarian resolution of a problem brings the unwanted side effects of increased resistance and lowered morale. In addition, splitting them up may spread the virus of resistance through the organization.

On the other hand, there should be beneficial ways to disperse their group solidarity. Think of providing an opportunity for each individual to change a personally destructive pattern. Maybe they're burned out or frustrated and need new opportunities. Perhaps their jobs don't mesh very well with their personal lives. Or maybe they need the challenge and stimulation of working with new people. You can find remedies, but whatever you decide on, make sure that you intend that it really help them.

If you tailor your actions individually, each member of the resistive group will end up with a different work situation. The specific actions are quite ordinary. Rearrange their work schedules or lunch times to fit their lives. Reposition work sites or allow individuals to work alone on satisfying projects. Assign them to different work teams where positive attitudes dominate. Or allow them transfers to other departments where they would prefer to work.

Timely firing has its place. Sometimes you have little choice but to neutralize a determined adversary who won't break off an attack. When you're *inviting* motivation and change, some people will refuse your invitation. If someone makes it clear he won't go along with a period of necessary change, you may have to fire him, after you've tried everything else. This challenge must be squarely faced. Everyone else, employees and supervisors, is watching. Backing off destroys crucial credibility.

But firing need not disrupt. According to John Chapman, "The rare times I've fired someone, there were clear-cut problems. I had an immediate meeting with staff, explained what I did, and got out their reactions. In the end, many came over to thank me, saying, 'It was about time.' Morale and productivity always jumped after these incidents. In effect, you're supporting the good employees by doing this."

Firing can also benefit the employee who is let go, releasing him from an untenable position, and providing him with an opportunity to find a more suitable work environment.

Of course, like anything else, make sure you don't overdo it. As a long-term strategy, motivation through firing loses more than it gains.

Select your spot. Better to fight with the sun at your back, and in the uphill rather than the downhill position. Similarly, start the change where some stress and strain exist, where there is already some dissatisfaction and openness to something new. Is there grumbling in one division? That's a perfect opportunity to pilot a system. Has an angry employee come to you to complain? It's the perfect time to reposition her.

Change organizational levels above and below target level. This is an example of indirect or secondary pressure (see chapter five). Want to encourage a supervisor to change? Shift her key subordinates or boss. Send them to a powerful training seminar. The heat will be on for the supervisor to shift also.

Overextend resistance. A punch's power can be neutralized by extending it a few inches beyond its target. In the same way, "giving enough rope" can allow a resistant employee to try things her way. If her approach fails, you can turn up the heat for change.

Make rewards. Link promotions and incentives to willingness and ability to change. The change-resistant person shouldn't get organizational approval. Just after a missed promotion, the employee may ask why he missed out. This is a golden moment; be honest with him. You may also initiate the conversation, but only do it in a spirit of personal concern.

Step 2: Changing

The student is convinced. He has thoroughly tested his teacher, whose techniques, as effortless as they appear, really do work. Now the beginner is past the skepticism that prevents learning.

The employee has put aside her resistance. Now you can help her find more effective approaches. Keep in mind her former resistance makes her a vulnerable learner. This period is one of trial and error and is often frustrating. Stay in close contact. This is the right time to provide appropriate training.

Find ways to help them learn new patterns:

- Introduce change as an experimental approach. Master martial arts instructors encourage exploration and so do accomplished change agents. This is much less threatening than asking people to commit themselves permanently to a new style: "We'll try it out temporarily to see how it works. Perhaps we can reassess the results in three months?"
  Give employees adequate time to get accustomed to the new ways. Then resistance to change may work for you; they'll most likely want to continue this method that will have become part of their routine.

- Provide models. Employees learn very quickly when they can model their movements after an expert. For instance, they can observe how peers perform effectively in similar situations. Or they may experiment with several different approaches. Being specific helps; define what new behaviour and attitudes you are looking for.

- Be a resource. In the martial arts, students learn more from feeling than from hearing or seeing. Yes, tell them what to do. But also show them and let them feel the technique. Use it with them and let them perform it successfully with you. They'll learn most quickly this way.

  Offer techniques such as mental rehearsal to whoever is interested. Provide them with appropriate reading matter that supports their change.

Step 3: Refreezing

When a martial arts student becomes a black belt, he's become an independent learner. After a change, we want to wean the employee from being dependent and increase his independence. After all of his efforts and ours, we don't want him to fall back into old patterns. He should be able to sustain the change on his own. Here are some strategies for anchoring (or refreezing) employees:

- Let them change. Control your own mind; think of them in their new light, not as formerly troublesome employees. Remember how graceful they've become. Don't treat them as the clumsy, resistant persons they were.

  In most organizations, there are employees who would like to change a previously well-deserved reputation. Many have difficulty shedding their old image because of colleagues who aren't willing or able to give them a chance to be different. Speak with the employee's work group and supervisor. Mention the fine efforts and progress she has made.

  Sometimes sending the employee away helps—on a leave, short off-site project, or training seminar. It breaks the negative relationship balance between the employee and her peers and provides them both with the opportunity to recast their expectations.

- Support them. Let them know how well they've done. Publicly acknowledge the target employee's accomplishments.

- Recall the important role they play in the organizational mission, and suggest a personal mission statement.

- Help them manage the stress from change. Exercise and the personal control techniques in the first section of this book can help.

DEFEND YOURSELF

Change happens gradually. Bruce Lee wrote, "The control of our being is not unlike the combination of a safe. One turn of the knob rarely unlocks the safe; each advance is a step toward one's final achievement."

Let's review some vital points. During a change process, there is often some fear and negativity. Keep your antennae tuned. Clear discontent from the air early by bringing it out in the open (at group or individual meetings); don't leave this to fester. Change is complex and rarely linear. Persistent patience and a long-term perspective are the change agent's best weapons.

Remember that you never really change others. You may invite them to act differently, but they are perfectly free to refuse your invitation. And you are equally free, after a firm refusal, to replace the employee. However, be sure to give your best efforts before you turn to this act of last resort.

Finally, the simplest actions can make large differences. Don't underestimate the power of thanking people. Courtesy and an understanding of inner motivation can induce great change.

Becoming an Agent of Change: Techniques for Action

- See where and how staff resist your role as a change agent.

- Watch your intent. Before any strong action, ask yourself: Am I wielding the sword that kills or the sword that preserves life?

- Look for opportunities to foster support and trust in your organization.

- Where are the kuzushi (imbalance) points in your organization?

- Discern when to "disturb" and when to "break" someone's balance. Change means shifting balance. Disturb resistant employees' balance and move them into a stronger position.

- Who is on the centreline in your organization? How does this change over time and with different issues?

- Look to develop others as change agents. If you approach them properly, you can enlist expert staff, vocal complainers, or those you wish to help grow.

- Restore the balance after any change.

- Use appropriate reigi (courtesy) to make a strong connection. Observe whether strong connection was ever made in poorly managed changes. Connection reduces resistance.

- Recognize what makes it harder and easier for your staff to change.

- Select environments that reduce threat and support change.

- Reduce fear of the unknown. Share as much of your battle plans as you reasonably can.

- Use "belt ceremonies" or milestones during a change.

- Get the most from any failure by using it as a vehicle for change. How can you see resistance melted, change modelled, and strong adaptations "refrozen"?

CONCLUSION

The Next Step: The Warrior's Approach

Real life managerial expertise won't come just from reading this or any other book.

There is a story of Aikido founder Morihei Ueshiba, who happened upon his student (now a master) Mitsugi Saotome, reading Musashi's *A Book of Five Rings*. Ueshiba remonstrated with him: "Listen closely to me, Saotome. Reading books will never polish your character, nor will they give you wisdom. Wisdom can only come through experience."

Realization—the "Aha! I've got it!"—is both art and science. It is emotional and physical as well as intellectual. Wisdom comes through doing. Action heightens clear thinking and is the proof of understanding.

Black belts are action oriented. Bruce Lee said it clearly: "Action is our relationship to everything." But calm action only emerges out of a relaxed spirit, a controlled attitude, and relentless preparation. Frantic, ill-conceived action is frequently worse than none at all.

Focus on changing yourself first. If you wish to create change, become a working gear; others you touch will also begin to move.

How long do you have to train? Real life is not like school; you don't finish the term, graduate, and end your study. Black-belt managing means continuous honing.

Beginning students often think they comprehend a technique, yet they can't make it work. Their actions show that they don't really understand. Similarly, at work, people often say, "Yes, I see," and continue to perform in ineffective ways. They have not fully understood, either. In *The Zen Way To the Martial Arts,* Taisen Deshimaru emphasizes, "You have to practise until you die."

It is said of jujitsu that it would require ten years of practice in order to win victory over one's self and twenty years to win victory over others.

Black-belt managers don't rest on their laurels; they continue to improve. Describing his year-long mapping project, John Chapman said, "When I sensed things were going well, I realized that it was time to listen more."

Maintaining a realistic perspective will protect you from unrealistic expectations. Yes, you can develop many powers, but think realistically. Be wary of being seduced by tall tales and simplistic answers. People are complex and the mastery of any art is broad and deep. Deshimaru wrote, "Do not be narrow-minded, always looking for rules and recipes. Every situation requires its own reaction."

Shodan, first degree black belt, literally means "first step" in Japanese. The meaning is clear. Learning the basics makes you a good beginner, not an expert.

Sometimes growing knowledge is accompanied by an inflating ego. New black belts, puffed up with pride, are usually asked to work out with their instructors, who give them a sound beating to pound out false pride.

You have learned, yes, but there is much ahead. Don't get lost. Work hard. And congratulations.

Worth is shown only in action. Notice what you do, what you really practise, and the precedents you set for yourself and others. Seek ongoing activities that develop your powers. Remember who you really are, what you have already accomplished, and what you are capable of. Then you can dedicate yourself to forging a high-performance, high-morale organization.

So, if we are always to be learning as managers, what is the best attitude to take and what should our expectations be? Swordsmaster Tesshu is quoted in his biography, *The Sword of No-Sound* by John Stevens: "In order not to develop improper habits, strive with your entire being. Forcefully and without restraint, swing the sword over and over. Extend yourself to the fullest, and concentrate on executing the techniques naturally. Eventually, real strength will be fostered; all stiffness will vanish and the techniques can be performed in a free-flowing manner. The opponent's movement can be detected before he strikes—one intuitively knows where to cut and any attack can be repelled. Have no confused thoughts or doubts, do not distort the techniques: without delay, train harder and harder!"

You can unlock the secrets of living and working with greater power, control, and creativity. Being calm under pressure, engendering high performance, feeling your rightful place in the world—these powers can increasingly be yours.

See, reflect, practise, and adjust. You will inevitably become a black belt in the art of managing.

GLOSSARY OF MARTIAL ARTS TERMS

aikido "The Way of harmonious forces," a twentieth-century Japanese martial art, developed by Morihei Ueshiba; it is a "soft" style, purely defensive, that utilizes minimal force to throw an attacker

aikijujitsu "Blending forces [mental and physical, yours and your opponents'] style of jujitsu," a Japanese martial art

budo Japanese term for the martial arts

bushido Japanese term for the way of the warrior

chi The Chinese term for inner energy, life force

defusing Helping to lower the energy in a conflict situation

displacement Separating yourself from a conflict, avoiding, etc.

do Japanese term for Way of life

double-weighted Weight evenly divided between both feet, a state which martial artists try to avoid because it reduces the ability to move quickly

gi (pronounced "gee" as in geese) Martial arts loose-fitting practice uniform, usually white or black

hapkido "Way of combining forces," a Korean martial art that emphasizes circular movements, kicks, and arm controls

hara The body's centre of gravity, located within the lower abdomen, life centre (believed to distribute *chi* to the rest of the body)

hsing-I "The Form of mind boxing," an open-armed, circular-movement Chinese martial art.

jeet kune do Martial art developed by Bruce Lee, who dubbed it "the formless form," emphasizing timing and position, economical movements, and strong hand defence.

jiuwaza Japanese term for free-form defence, in martial arts, not having any specific technique.

judo "The Way of yielding," a Japanese martial art developed in the twentieth century by Prof. Jigoro Kano

jujitsu The "Science of combat through yielding," a Japanese martial art, forerunner of judo; focus is on leverage, using an opponent's strength against him (to throw him)

ka (suffix) Practitioner, player (as in *judoka*)

karate "The empty fist" or "open hand," an Okinawan-Japanese martial art, modernized by Gichin Funakoshi

kata Stylized martial arts forms in which the practitioner defends against invisible multiple attackers from all directions; also the word for a practice form

kenpo or *kempo* Chinese karate emphasizing circular movements

kendo The Way of the sword, Japanese martial art

kenjutsu The Japanese art of swordsmanship

ki Same as *chi* (Japanese term)

ki-ai Martial arts shout (Japanese term) designed for focusing your *ki* into a strong movement (punch, kick) or for momentarily freezing an opponent

kiaijitsu Martial art that employs the voice as a weapon; with this art it is said that masters are able to kill birds with one strong shout

kiyop Korean term, same as ki-ai

kung fu "The supreme technique," a family of Chinese martial arts emphasizing internal development

kuzushi Point of unbalance, one of eight around the standing body

kyudo "The Way of the bow," the modern martial art of archery practises with targets; its forerunner, *kyujitsu*, was used in combat

misogi breath Purification technique through breathing

motorset A stage (usually in conflict) where a person is on edge, ready to go

ninja One who practises ninjisu, formerly practised in secret by families who would perform assassinations by contract *ninjitsu* Martial art employing stealth

nunchaku Japanese weapon made up of two sticks joined by a chain

obi Belt, sash; the coloured belt that holds closed a martial artist's gi

pa-kua "Boxing," Chinese martial art

parry Deflect an incoming strike without directly blocking it

positive space During an attack, the area it is safe to move into

samurai Japanese warrior, literally, "one who serves"

sensei Instructor, literally, "one who is born before"

Shaolin Sect of Chinese monks who developed a style of kung fu

shidare yanagi-ryu See yanagi-ryu

shihan Master

shinai Bamboo sword used in martial arts practice

shodan First degree black belt, literally, "first step"

shuto Knifehand strike; "karate chop"

suki An opening, a moment of opportunity to act

tae kwon do "The foot-fist way," Korean martial art; emphasis is on powerful kicking

t'ai chi ch'uan "Supreme ultimate boxing," Chinese martial art, practised by the slow repetition of forms to develop balance and concentration

tao te ching "The Way of Life," book written by Lao Tsu in the fifth century B.C.; focus is on how to live wisely in accordance with natural forces and how to lead others

untargetting Positioning yourself so as not to directly receive a verbal attack

wa Inner harmony

waza Japanese term for technique

yanagi-ryu Style of aikijujitsu (full name is *shidare yanagi ryu:* "weeping willow style," from the observation that in the storm, the oak tree that resists is uprooted, whereas the firmly rooted willow yields to the gale and springs back into place when the storm passes

BIBLIOGRAPHY

Martial Arts Sources

Chung-liang Huang, Al. *Embrace Tiger, Return To Mountain: The Essence of Tai Chi.* Moab, Utah: Real People Press, 1973.

Cosmé, Cassandra and Barry. "Ki Redefined: The Ability To Make a Clear Decision," *Black Belt,* Vol. 18 (April, 1980), pp. 26–29.

Deshimaru, Taisen. *The Zen Way to the Martial Arts,* trans. Nancy Amphoux. New York: E. P. Dutton, 1982.

Funakoshi, Gichin. *Karate-do: My Way of Life.* Tokyo: Kodansha International Ltd.,1975.

Hayes, Stephen. *Wisdom From the Ninja Village of the Cold Moon.* Chicago: Contemporary Books, 1984.

Herrigel, Eugen. *Zen in the Art of Archery.* New York: Vintage Books, 1971

Huard, Pierre and Ming Wong. *Oriental Methods of Mental and Physical Fitness.* New York, Funk & Wagnalls, 1977.

Hyams, Joe. *Zen in the Martial Arts.* Los Angeles: J. P. Tarcher Inc., 1979.

Inosanto, Dan. *The Filipino Martial Arts.* Los Angeles: Know How Publishing Co., 1980.

Kammer, Richard. *Zen and Confucius in the Art of Swordsmanship: The Tengu-Geijutsu-Ton of Chozan Shissai.* London: Routledge & Kegan Paul, London & Henley, 1978.

Kauz, Herman. *The Martial Spirit: An Introduction to the Origin, Philosophy, and Psychology of the Martial Arts.* Woodstock, N.Y.: The Overlook Press, 1977.

Kim, Ashida. *Ninja Mind Control.* New York: Berkley Books, 1987.

———. *Ninja Secrets of Invisibility.* Secaucus, N. J.: Citadel Press, 1983.

Kubota, Tak. *The Art of Karate.* New York: Peebles Press, 1977.

Lee, Bruce. *The Tao of Jeet Kune Do.* Burbank, Ca.: Ohara Publications, 1975.

Lerner, Ira. *Diary of the Way: Three Paths to Enlightenment.* New York: Ridge Press, 1976.

Liang, T.T. *T'ai Chi Ch'uan for Health and Self-defense.* Boston: Redwing Book Company, 1974.

Maslak, Paul. *Strategy in Unarmed Conflict.* Burbank, Ca.: Unique Publications, 1980.

Mukoh (Tr). *Hagakure: A Code to the Way of the Samurai.* Heian, 1981.

Muryasz, Walter. *Precepts of the Martial Artist.* San Diego: General Integration, 1984.

Musashi, Miyamoto. *A Book of Five Rings.* trans. Victor Harris. Woodstock, N.Y.: The Overlook Press, 1974.

———. *The Book of Five Rings.* trans. Nihon Service Corporation. New York: Bantam Books, 1982.

Okazaki, Henry Seishiro. "The Esoteric Principles of Judo." unpublished paper.

Parker, Ed. *Secrets of Chinese Karate.* New York: Funk & Wagnalls, 1963.

Random, Michel. *The Martial Arts,* trans. Judy Boothroyd. London: Octopus Books Ltd., 1978.

Saotome, Mitsugi. *Aikido and the Harmony of Nature.* France: Sedirep, 1986.

Smith, Robert. *Hsing-I: Chinese Mind-Body Boxing.* Tokyo: Kodansha International, Ltd., 1974.

———. *Pa-Kua: Chinese Boxing For Fitness and Self-defense.* San Francisco: Kodansha International Ltd., 1974.

Stevens, John. *The Sword of No-Sword: Life of the Master Warrior Tesshu.* Boston: Shambhala Publications, 1986.

Sun Tzu. *The Art of War,* trans. Samuel B. Griffith. London: Oxford University Press, 1971.

Suzuki, Daisetz. *Zen and Japanese Culture.* Princeton: Princeton University Press, 1973.

Ueshiba, Kisshomaru. *Aikido.* Tokyo: Hozansha Publishing Co., Ltd., 1974.

Wilson, William Scott, trans. *Hagakure: The Book of the Samurai.* Tokyo: Kodansha, 1978.

———. ed. and trans. *Ideals of the Samurai: Writings of Japanese Warriors.* Burbank, Ca.: Ohara Publications, 1982.

Management Books

Cooper, Cary and Judi Marshall. *Understanding Executive Stress.* Princeton: Petrocelli, 1978.

Deal, Terrence E. and Allan A. Kennedy. *Corporate Cultures: The Rites and Rituals of Corporate Life.* Reading, Ma.: Addison-Wesley, 1982.

Fitch, Donald. *Increasing Productivity in the Microcomputer Age.* Reading, Ma.: Addison-Wesley, 1982.

Gibb, Jack. *Trust: A New View of Personal and Organizational Development.* Los Angeles: Guild of Tutors Press, 1978.

Grove, Andrew. *High Output Management.* New York: Random House, 1983.

Gruneberg, Michael. *Understanding Job Satisfaction.* London: The MacMillan Press, 1979.

Herzberg, Frederick. *Work and the Nature of Man.* Cleveland: World Press, 1966.

Hultman, Ken. *The Path of Least Resistance: Preparing Employees for Change.* Austin, Tex.: Learning Concepts, 1979.

Lewin, Kurt. *Field Theory in the Social Sciences.* New York: Harpers, 1953.

Maslow, Abraham. *Motivation and Personality.* New York: Harper & Row, 1954.

Ohmae, Kenichi. *The Mind of the Strategist: Business Planning for Competitive Advantage.* New York: Penguin Books, 1983.

Pascale, Richard T. and Anthony G. Athos. *The Art of Japanese Management: Applications for American Executives.* New York: Bantam Books, 1979.

Peters, Tom and Robert Waterman. *In Search of Excellence.* New York: Harper & Row, 1982.

Prince, George M. *The Practice of Creativity: A Manual for Dynamic Group Problem Solving.* New York: Collier, 1970.

Townsend, Robert. *Further Up the Organization.* New York: Alfred A. Knopf, 1984.

Miscellaneous Readings

Burroughs, William. "The Discipline of D. E.," in *The Exterminator.* New York: Penguin Books, 1985.

Gallwey, W. Timothy. *The Inner Game of Tennis.* New York: Bantam Books, 1979.

Kappas, John. *Professional Hypnotism Manual,* revised ed. Alhambra, Ca.: Borden, 1978.

Lao Tsu. *Tao Te Ching: The Way of Life,* trans. Witter Bynner. New York: Perigree Books, 1980.

von Oech, Roger. *A Whack on the Side of the Head: How to Unlock Your Mind for Innovation.* New York: Warner Books, 1983.

Watzlawick, Paul. *How Real Is Real: Confusion, Disinformation, and Communication.* New York: Random House, 1977.

INDEX